WILLIAM WILBERFORCE

Abolitionist, Politician, Writer

Lon Fendall

BARBOUR BOOKS

An Imprint of Barbour Publishing, Inc.

Other books in the "Heroes of the Faith" series:

Brother Andrew	Samuel Morris
Gladys Aylward	George Müller
Dietrich Bonhoeffer	Watchman Nee
William and Catherine Booth	John Newton
John Bunyan	Florence Nightingale
John Calvin	Luis Palau
William Carey	Francis and Edith Schaeffer
Amy Carmichael	Charles Sheldon
George Washington Carver	Mary Slessor
Fanny Crosby	Charles Spurgeon
Frederick Douglass	John and Betty Stam
Jonathan Edwards	Billy Sunday
Jim Elliot	Hudson Taylor
Charles Finney	William Tyndale
Billy Graham	Corrie ten Boom
C. S. Lewis	Mother Teresa
Eric Liddell	Sojourner Truth
David Livingstone	John Wesley
Martin Luther	George Whitefield
D. L. Moody	John Wycliffe

Published by Barbour Books, an imprint of Barbour Publishing, Inc., P.O. Box 719, Uhrichsville, OH 44683 http://www.barbourbooks.com

Cover illustration © Dick Bobnick.

Member of the
Evangelical Christian
Publishers Association

Printed in the United States of America.

WILLIAM WILBERFORCE

one

I have good news for you, William," said Thomas
Macaulay, one of William Wilberforce's longtime
friends. "God has answered your prayers and brought
victory in your life's struggle."

"Yes, I heard about the vote in Parliament to eliminate slavery in the empire. I've been thanking God since
the word came." Wilberforce refused to take any credit
for himself, however. Countless people had labored for
years to reach this goal, and the victory was God's.
Besides, victory was yet to come for those still enslaved
in the United States of America and many other places
in the world.

Macaulay felt certain that his friend did not have long
to live, so the victory must be sweet for him, despite his
humility. Wilberforce's body had been weakened by

numerous ailments, but it was apparent that William Wilberforce still possessed a keen mind and was fully aware of what was happening in the world. He had so much to teach! Macaulay settled back in his chair and encouraged his friend to share some of his life experiences.

"What's wrong, Macaulay? Don't you think I'm going to live much longer? Well, if you have the time, so do I. Will you promise to stop me if I tell you more than you want to know?"

One of William's grandsons brought tea and biscuits for the two men and checked to make sure the aging Wilberforce was comfortable. The sun streamed in through the curtains in the house where the Wilberforce family was staying to be near medical care.

Wilberforce had been well into his political career before he saw any need to surrender his life to Christ as Savior and Lord. He had been elected to the seat from Hull when he was barely old enough to serve. Then the opportunity came to move up a bit and win one of the seats from Yorkshire, which was about twenty times as large as Hull. On March 25, 1784, the Yorkshire Association called a meeting of the voters of the district to solicit support for reforms in Parliament and get more backing for Prime Minister William Pitt. Wilberforce went to York to help out the cause of his friend Pitt, whom he had known from Cambridge and had been working with in the House of Commons. No one at the York meeting, including Wilberforce, expected that the day would end with his being positioned as a likely choice for one of the two Yorkshire seats.

The amazing thing about the rally at York was that

four thousand voters showed up, even though it was a miserably cold day. Not only did they show up, but they stayed through the whole day to hear the various speakers. The organizers of the meeting wanted the group to adopt a petition to the king, asking for an immediate election. This tactic was meant to give prominence to the reform goals of the Yorkshire Association and help William Pitt's supporters win seats in the House of Commons.

The speeches continued on through the afternoon. It seemed that all the important people in Yorkshire had been given a chance. Wilberforce's district of Hull was within Yorkshire, even though it was separate for the purpose of representation in Commons; so some of his constituents were there that day, but no one thought he would be given an opportunity to speak. At about 4:00 P.M., his turn finally came. It was not much of an honor to be given the platform when the crowd was tired, cold, and restless, so Wilberforce half expected most of the people would leave before he could get much said. To his surprise, the people became quiet and listened to him. Wilberforce held their attention for nearly an hour.

When he was about to bring his speech to a close, Wilberforce saw a commotion on the edge of the crowd. He thought at first it was a group starting to head home but soon realized that a messenger from the king was trying to reach the platform. Wilberforce motioned him forward and took it on himself to read the message. Then he announced that the king had dissolved Parliament the day before and the election was going to happen in the near future. He called on the group to join forces behind the efforts for reform and to assure that Prime Minister Pitt would be able to continue giving his strong leadership. Not only was there great support in the crowd for this proposition, but some in the crowd began to shout out that Wilberforce should be considered for one of Yorkshire's two seats. Prior to that, he was a literal unknown in most of Yorkshire, but within days a canvass was held, and he got one of the seats.

"God works in amazing ways, even for those who don't acknowledge Him. Don't you ever forget that, Macaulay," Wilberforce admonished his friend.

Macaulay leaned forward with his next question. "Was your conversion experience as dramatic as your selection to the Yorkshire seat in Commons?"

"No, it was not dramatic at all," Wilberforce replied. "If you're hoping to hear about something like the apostle Paul's conversion on the road to Damascus, you are going to be disappointed." Wilberforce smiled. "Actually, my spiritual rebirth did happen on a road, but there was no blinding light or voice from God. It was on the road to and from the Riviera that God began to speak to me."

It had been important that Wilberforce accompany his mother, sister, and two cousins on their way to the coast of France. The trip required a long carriage ride to the port, a passage by ship across the Channel, then another carriage ride to Nice. Even though Wilberforce had plenty to attend to in his new duties representing Yorkshire, it would have been unthinkable to send the ladies off without a male escort to look after their needs.

Wilberforce had had difficulty finding a male friend to

accompany them—someone he could talk to on the way and who would help with the arrangements. He was getting a little desperate, so he asked someone he didn't know very well—Isaac Milner, a lecturer at Cambridge who had been a teacher at the primary school Wilberforce had attended. He knew Milner was a very bright person and thought they would have many interesting things to talk about during the trip.

What he didn't know was that Milner had become what Wilberforce and his friends scoffingly called a "methodist." Wilberforce and his friends felt that these methodists, or evangelicals, were way off the track. They talked about the need for a conversion experience quite apart from one's baptism into the church as a child. That seemed ridiculous to Wilberforce. Besides, the evangelicals seemed to put way too much emphasis on emotionalism. Religion to Wilberforce was a part of one's social obligations. He had no great problem with the sermons he heard in church, but the talk about Jesus forgiving one's sins seemed totally absurd.

"So, William, did Isaac Milner try to convert you to his type of evangelical faith?" Macaulay asked.

"Not really. He didn't even bring up the subject."

Wilberforce's favorite theologian at the time was Theophilus Lindsey, who was the first in the Church of England to talk about God as one being, not the Trinity. Unitarianism sounded great to a young intellectual who didn't want to deal with the many supernatural things in the New Testament.

Along the way, Wilberforce picked up a copy of a book by Philip Doddridge. He asked Milner what he thought of the book, and Milner said it was one of the best he had ever read. Milner and Wilberforce read it together and talked about it on the way home to England, and Wilberforce began to realize the truth of the gospel. But he was still not ready to make a commitment.

Isaac Milner agreed to accompany Wilberforce back to France to bring the women home at the end of the season. On the way, they discussed the Bible and what it means to be a follower of Christ. They read and discussed the New Testament in Greek, since both of them had studied the language at Cambridge. There actually was no single moment at which Wilberforce prayed for the forgiveness of his sins and asked Jesus to be his Savior. It happened to him over a period of months. Gradually he began to turn his back on his frivolous ways and began to meditate, pray, and write his thoughts and questions in a journal. By the end of the year, he had become a serious follower of Christ.

"May I prevail on you to tell me about one other great event in your life, the victory in Parliament over slavery in the British Empire?" asked Macaulay.

"Certainly. The success of that effort is the result of the work of many people. I did what I could before retiring from Parliament—and even after that—but others deserve most of the credit."

"Why didn't you just go ahead and work for the abolition of slavery back in 1807, instead of settling for a bill that outlawed British participation in the slave trade?"

Almost all of those involved in the abolition movement would have preferred to take care of the slavery problem all at once. They had worked in the cause for more than twenty years and had no desire to drag it out for another twenty-five, but in politics one has to settle for modest steps toward accomplishing a larger goal. As strong as the support for slavery was, they would never have succeeded in passing emancipation in 1807. They had to settle for putting an end to the trade and trust that the public conscience would begin to understand that slavery itself was the evil, not just slave trafficking.

On the night the abolition bill passed, Wilberforce hardly said a word in Parliament. Most of their efforts had been in the House of Commons, but in this case some very clever planning in the House of Lords led to the tactic of attaching an abolition measure to another bill that was expected to get the support of the proslavery forces. It worked, removing the possibility of the House of Lords' blocking action at a later time.

When the discussion proceeded in Commons, it seemed almost anticlimactic; government ministers backed the abolition measure. So dramatic was the shift toward support of the measure, only sixteen members voted against it. Wilberforce couldn't believe his ears when the vote was announced. He went home early that morning with inexpressible joy that he had been able to see the first major victory in the greatest of his life callings. He gave all the glory to God that night. "Praise His name for putting it into the hearts of our politicians to finally do the right thing," Wilberforce said.

two

"Welcome, young Willy! We are so pleased that you have come to live with us. Hannah and I will do our best to make you feel at home."

The warm welcome from his uncle William and aunt Hannah was comforting to nine-year-old William Wilberforce. Tragedy seemed everywhere recently. Just the year before, his sister Elizabeth had died at the age of fourteen. Elizabeth had been away at a boarding school for most of Willy's growing-up years, but he had treasured the times she was home.

Soon after the death of his sister, Willy lost his father, Robert Wilberforce, who was only forty when he died. Robert had been in the family businesses of banking and trade with Europe. Willy hadn't felt very close to his father, but the loss of two of his immediate family members in a few months had been difficult. Dealing with the death of his loved ones made William even more conscious of his own physical limitations. He was slight of build, not at all strong, and had poor eyesight.

Robert and Hannah felt more than pity for the young boy who came to join their household. God had not blessed them with children of their own, so they were delighted to have Willy to love and care for. They saw a boy with a strong mind that made up for his weak body. They were impressed with his wit and his ability to express himself far better than one would expect from a boy of nine. They hoped they could provide some important spiritual nurture for him, too.

After tea was served and Willy's things delivered to his new room at the spacious Wilberforce house on St. James Place, Willy's uncle spoke of the plans he and Hannah had made for him. They had spoken to Mr. Chambers, head-master at Putney School, and were assured there was a place for Willy at the school. Willy had done well at Hull Grammar School, particularly because of the teaching of young Joseph Milner. They assured their nephew that the teachers at Putney would be able to challenge his mind, and he would make many friends there. He would have classes in writing, French, arithmetic, Latin, and a little Greek. "You have a great future in the Wilberforce family businesses, young man," Uncle William promised.

"Uncle William, I remember coming to visit you at your place in Wimbledon. I loved being in your garden. I can still hear the birds singing. Can we go there soon?"

"Well, there's not enough time right now. We've got to get you settled at school. But we'll all go there during the holidays. God has blessed us very much, and we want to do

14

everything to make you happy. And, yes, there are still birds at Wimbledon."

Almost two weeks had passed since Willy arrived in London, and he knew he had to write to his mother, Elizabeth.

Dearest Mum, he began the letter.

> *Uncle and Auntie have been very kind to me, and I'm doing well. They send you their love. I like my room at their house on St. James Place, and they have promised we will go to Wimbledon during the first holiday. Maybe you can join us there. I wish I could say I liked my school, but that would not be true. The classes are not nearly as interesting as those at Hull, and the food makes me ill. There is this despicable man on the school staff who is supposed to keep us in order. He's Scottish, and he seems intent on showing us that we English are somehow inferior to the Scots. But I suppose I'll be okay, Mum. I miss you. Give my love to Sarah and give an extra hug to Ann. Aunt Hannah is going to come for me next weekend. She said we would go to visit her brother, John Thornton, at Clapham. There is a church there she says I will enjoy. Bye, for now.*
>
> Your loving son,
Willy.

Other letters followed as Willy adapted to his new life.

15

Dearest Mum,

My visit to Hull was grand. Mum, you remember when I first arrived more than a year ago, I told you about going with Aunt Hannah to her brother's church in Clapham? We've gone there several times since. Some of the people there call themselves "Methodists," but I'm not quite sure what that means. I suspect you might not like some of the things they are teaching in their church.

We went to church at Clapham again last Sunday, and the guest minister was very interesting. His name is John Newton. He's the rector at Olney in Buckinghamshire. For a parson, he has had a most amazing life. He talked about his days at sea and how God had delivered him from terrible circumstances. He became captain of a slave ship, but now he has asked God to forgive him for being so cruel to the people of Africa. He said he had come to understand that slavery was sinful and had asked God to forgive him for his past and to help him treat people more lovingly. He made me want to commit my life to Jesus. I hope you can come to hear him preach sometime.

> *Until later, your loving son,*
> *Willy.*

Willy's mother greeted her father-in-law on a cold, drizzly day in Hull. "I'm so glad you've come. Let's go inside and have tea. I must read you the letter I just got from Willy in London. I'm so concerned that he seems to have taken up

16

with the Enthusiasts in Clapham that William and Hannah admire so much. I just don't think I dare leave him there any longer. I'd like to know what you think."

Elizabeth was a loyal member of the Church of England, at least at a social level. She and others of wealth disdained both the theology and the social class of the followers of John Wesley. Two decades before Willy's birth, John Wesley, himself a loyal member of the Church of England, had a profound spiritual experience. He spoke of his heart being "strangely warmed" and of trusting in Christ for salvation. He believed that his sins had been forgiven by faith alone, not by his baptism as a child. At the time Willy was attending services in Clapham, the name "Methodist" was used interchangeably with the term "Enthusiast"—a person who was far too emotional about his or her spirituality and put too much emphasis on salvation and forgiveness of sins. An even greater problem for Elizabeth Wilberforce was the fact that most Methodists were from the lower classes.

William and Hannah were close friends of George Whitefield, who was making quite an impression on people of wealth. Elizabeth didn't think Willy had heard Whitefield preach, but John Newton was a Methodist, and his talk of forgiveness from sins, personal salvation, and faith alone went against all she had learned in the church about the sacraments and the baptism of children as the way to confirm one's faith.

"You're right, Elizabeth," said her father-in-law, William. "Your son carries my name, and he won't get a penny of my inheritance if he continues down this Methodist pathway. William and Hannah won't like it if

17

you take him from their care, but you really must. There's so much at stake for the future of our family. How disgusting it would be for Willy to become a Methodist!"

It was very quiet on the coach ride home to Hull. The emotions of the abrupt departure were heavy. Willy tried not to show his sadness and anger as he thought about the terrible scene when his mother arrived and informed his aunt and uncle that she was going to take Willy back to Hull. He desperately wished he hadn't written to his mother about John Newton's sermons at Clapham and his own seeking of the spiritual rebirth that had attracted him to the Methodists' message. He should have known how his mother and grandfather would react, since they so despised what they considered the spiritual excesses of the lower classes.

He struggled for words. "Mother, I know you don't like the fact that I was interested in the Methodists. But you saw how Uncle William and Aunt Hannah were devastated by my having to leave. They have no children of their own. I've gotten used to the school at Putney. If I promise not to go back to the church at Clapham, could I return to live with Uncle and Auntie?"

"Of course not, Child. You have no idea what it would do to your future as a member of the Wilberforce family if you continued with this Methodist nonsense. Your father would have been shocked by what you've done and said. I owe it to him to rescue you from these terrible influences."

"Can I go back to Hull School? I really liked that school."

"Absolutely not, Child. The new headmaster, Joseph Milner, has become a Methodist. It's already been arranged. You will go to your grandfather's old school at Pocklington.

The headmaster is Rev. Kingsman Baskett, and I'm sure he will not tolerate any Methodism at the school."

Nothing about the forced relocation to Pocklington School was to the liking of twelve-year-old William Wilberforce. He missed the affection and spiritual nurture of his aunt and uncle. He wrote words of encouragement to his uncle that reflected his own loneliness and spiritual discouragement: "Comfort yourself, you Dearest, that they who are in Jesus must suffer Persecution and it is just as it should be; if we suffer with Him we shall also reign with Him; and let what will happen he is blessed who has the Lord for his hope, who can look unto Him as unto a loving father being reconciled to Him by the blood of Jesus."[1]

Young William later said of the school at Pocklington, "The master was a good sort of man and rather an elegant scholar, but the boys were a sad set. . . . I did nothing at all there."[2]

The voids in Wilberforce's intellectual and spiritual life during his five years at Pocklington School were gradually filled with his increased access to the wealth of his family and the abundant social opportunities in Hull. While not measuring up to London, some called Hull the "Dublin of England" because of its many theaters, balls, lavish dinners, and card parties. During school holidays, Willy's life consisted of a daily routine of dinner at two, tea at six, card playing until nine, then a lavish supper. Willy's grandfather died during this time, and since Willy had by all appearances left his Methodism behind, his grandfather left him a more than comfortable inheritance. The abundance of money and leisure time made Willy a favored social companion, as did his conversational skills and his remarkable singing voice.

The fading of Wilberforce's earlier spiritual interests was of his own doing, but he had plenty of help. He later said of this process:

> *As grandson of one of the principal inhabi-*
> *tants, I was everywhere invited and caressed: My*
> *voice and love of music made me still more*
> *acceptable. The religious impressions that I*
> *gained at Wimbledon continued for a consider-*
> *able time, but my friends spared no pains to stifle*
> *them. I might almost say that no pious parent*
> *ever laboured more to impress a beloved child*
> *with sentiments of piety than they did to give me*
> *a taste of the world and its diversions.*[3]

Wilberforce's preference for social activities over academic and spiritual development continued after he was admitted to St. John's College, Cambridge University. Given the social standing of his family and his completion of studies at a well-known school, it was not hard for Wilberforce to get into Cambridge. Once there, he discovered that a person of means could get along well at the university without letting studies interfere with his social life. Only those headed into careers in the law and the clergy were pushed toward intellectual rigor. He said of his initiation into life at Cambridge:

> *I was introduced, on the very first night of my*
> *arrival, to as licentious a set of men as can well*
> *be conceived. They drank hard, and their conver-*
> *sation was even worse than their lives. . . . But*

*those with whom I was intimate did not act
towards me the part of Christians, or even of honest men. Their object seemed to be to make and
keep me idle.*

Of course, Wilberforce made his own decisions about
the use of his time and energies at Cambridge and later
came to regret the decisions he made. But he regretted that
his tutors did nothing to discourage his idleness at the university. They apparently assumed he would finish at
Cambridge and slip into adulthood with all his material
needs met and without much need for intellectual depth.

As on many evenings, Wilberforce returned to his room
in St. John's, tired from a day of card playing, drinking,
eating, singing, and conversation. The word at the time for
witty repartee was "foining," and William got high marks
at Cambridge as a foinster.

It was late, but he didn't want to go to bed yet, so he
banged on the stove chimney in his room, summoning the
student next door, Thomas Gisborne.

"You're studying far too hard, Gisborne," a laughing
Wilberforce said. You're going to completely wear out that
brain of yours." Offering his neighbor a chair, Wilberforce
tried to tempt the studious Gisborne with Yorkshire pie and
ale. "You've already established yourself as one of our top
students," Wilberforce complimented. "Why study so hard?"

"I'm studying for the priesthood, and the examiners
can be very tough," Gisborne replied, adding wistfully that
he had not been blessed with the kind of money and business opportunities Wilberforce had. The ministry offered
Gisborne a secure position in the future, the chance to do

good for humanity, and the opportunity to honor God.

Still, the serious Gisborne recognized the appeal of Wilberforce's life of pleasure. "You have it made," he told his host. "You're bright. You're one of the most popular students in our college. You're a gifted speaker. You can sing. People love being around you."

Wilberforce paused for a moment as Gisborne's comments registered. "Perhaps," Wilberforce said thoughtfully. "But I envy your determination and your hard work. You know what? I have no real idea of where I'm headed in life."

Family businesses, with their comfortable incomes, awaited William Wilberforce if he chose to pursue them. But his heart wasn't in trade and banking. The world of politics was a possibility, all the more so since Wilberforce had met the energetic young William Pitt—a man starting a career that would one day lead to the prime minister's office. But Wilberforce had to admit that his own interest in politics lacked the clear direction that Pitt so obviously possessed.

"Well, William, I suspect you will find your purpose in life one of these days," Gisborne sighed. "Meanwhile, you're enjoying life immensely, or so it seems."

"I suppose it does seem so," William admitted.

But he really did not enjoy all the gambling, drinking, and banqueting as much as he thought he would. He felt seduced into a life of idleness, partially by his tutors and friends, who seemed determined to keep him from applying himself. He told Gisborne about his years with his aunt and uncle. "I had every intention of committing my life to Christ as Savior and Lord. I think I actually did so, as much as a young boy could. But that life of spiritual zeal seems very distant from me now. Well, Thomas, I'll not be blamed for keeping you from your studies as others have done to me. You will be going to lectures tomorrow. As you know, that's not my habit. Good night."

three

"Excuse me, Mr. Pitt. Do you mind if I join you?" Wilberforce asked as he searched for a seat in the gallery of the House of Commons. "We met at Cambridge, as I recall. I've seen you a number of times here in the gallery, and I suspect we may be here for the same reasons. Unless I'm mistaken, your goal is to be down there on the floor before long."

Pitt nodded. "I'm studying for the bar now. It's important that I take the exam before I get too far down the political road. You're from Hull, aren't you? Is that where you would stand for election?"

"Yes, but nobody there thinks of me as a political contender. I don't have the political heritage you have. What seat would you seek?"

"That's a problem. There's no logical place for me to

run. I suppose I'll try in Cambridge, but my youth will be a problem there. Are you twenty-one yet?"

"Not until next August. If I were good at prayer, I would pray that the elections wait until after my birthday."

"Timing is everything in politics, isn't it?" Pitt noted. "Well, it seems the members have exhausted their store of wisdom for the evening and are about to adjourn. Please join me in getting a bite to eat before we go home."

Wilberforce's entrance into politics was almost a random choice. The funds he inherited from his grandfather and uncle assured that he could be comfortable without additional income. Although he was the only son in his family and could have taken his father's place in the trading business, he had no interest in that career. There were cousins in the business who were more than happy to continue managing it.

William had not applied himself adequately at the university to study for the bar, and he had no interest in being a clergyman. Medicine was out of the question because of his grades. The remaining option for a person of his class was a career in politics, so that became his choice.

Wilberforce could not have come up with even a short list of issues that drew him into politics. People told him he was a good speaker. He was personable and popular, but he had a fairly limited understanding of the issues being debated in Parliament. He assumed he could become better informed with time, and toward that end he had been spending his time listening to the debates in Westminster Palace.

As Pitt said, in politics timing is everything. Although he wouldn't have given credit to God at the time,

Wilberforce couldn't have been better served by the announcement that Parliament was dissolved, and there would be new elections. Prime Minister Lord North actually made the dissolution announcement on Wilberforce's twenty-first birthday, assuring that he would be old enough to seek a seat in Parliament. Though he had no advance warning of the announcement, Wilberforce had already invited the people of Hull to help him celebrate his birthday at an ox roast.

It was common practice at the time to give cash payments to voters in exchange for their support. English political leaders viewed the practice as an expression of appreciation for those who intended to vote for them. The going rate was two guineas for a vote. Hull voters who lived in London and voted in Hull expected to receive ten guineas for the effort of coming home to cast their votes. The total cost for these payments and other campaign expenses was eight thousand pounds, a substantial sum for the average person, but Wilberforce had plenty of money to work with.

"Wilberforce, my friend, congratulations on your impressive victory at Hull!" Pitt exclaimed after the election. "I heard you got as many votes as the two incumbents combined."

"Yes, I worked fairly hard at meeting the voters. I'm sorry to hear that things didn't go as well for you in Cambridge. Are you in the process of arranging for a seat from one of the small boroughs?"

"Yes. You might as well call it what everyone does—a rotten borough. The person whose borough I will represent has assured me I can operate independently in the House. I hope things will work out in time for me to take my seat in January."

"Excellent, Pitt. There is much about politics I can learn from you, and I have no doubt that your career will be far more impressive than mine."

Wilberforce's prediction proved to be on the mark. From the time of Pitt's arrival in the House of Commons, he made a positive impression. He made an excellent first speech in the Commons on financial reform. Many agreed with Wilberforce's assessment that Pitt would soon be a contender for prime minister. Later Pitt speeches criticizing the government for its handling of the war in the colonies won additional acclaim. Wilberforce, meanwhile, lacked passion and had identified no major causes to address in his early days in Commons. He first spoke during the debate on a bill to control smuggling and next entered the debate on naval shipbuilding. Neither effort earned him a place in history. More importantly, he used his early years in Commons to build relationships with other members, to become familiar with legislative procedures, and to analyze the persuasive styles of the more effective members.

Wilberforce at first took his place with the Tories, the party of William Pitt. The Tories were associated with the effort to reform Parliament and were connected with the business interests more than their rivals, the Whigs, who were more often the aristocrats. In reality, the parties were far less important than they would be later, and Wilberforce was more loyal to Pitt than to the party as such.

One of Wilberforce's major challenges during the years he represented Hull was gaining acceptance into the social networks of London. His background as a member of a merchant and banking family was a liability in that regard. He had plenty of money but not the social standing enjoyed by the aristocracy. He set out to gain acceptance through the same assets that had made him popular at Cambridge—his wealth, his wit, his charm, his impressive speaking voice, and at times his impressive singing ability. In this process of building social relationships in national life, there was almost no substitute for actively participating in one or more of the "members-only" social clubs. There was where one forged friendships and established relationships of trust. There was where one could soften the opposition of those who might block one's efforts. There was where signals could be cleared and plans developed.

Two of the clubs were identified with the two major parties. The Tories tended to congregate at White's, while the Whigs favored Brook's. Wilberforce joined both White's and Brook's so he would be able to gain support from either party. Not needing to watch his pennies, he also joined Boodle's, Miles and Evans, and Goosetree's. The clubs helped Wilberforce form alliances for future battles. As a young single man, he essentially made the clubs his home, a place to pass the time pleasantly when not involved in the duties of office. For some club members the attraction was gambling. Wilberforce did his share of gambling for a time but decided to abstain from the compulsive gambling that financially ruined some club members.

After four years, Wilberforce was beginning to get a feel for how things got done in the House of Commons and had worked with Pitt on some major projects, but he didn't feel he had much to show for his four years of effort. He had strong support in Hull, but simply staying in office was not exactly a worthy goal in life. He knew a lot of people but felt he ought to be doing more than building friendships.

"Pitt, you did take care of obtaining a letter of introduction to the French officials in Rheims, didn't you?"

"I thought you were going to do that," replied Pitt.

Their traveling companion and friend Edward Eliot thought the situation was extremely funny as they traveled across the English Channel with no idea of how they would make connections in France to assure they would be treated with cordiality and respect. The trip across the Channel went well, the three found adequate lodging, and Pitt proceeded to find someone willing to write the appropriate letter introducing them as well-placed English visitors who should be extended every courtesy while visiting France.

Unfortunately, Abbé de Lageard, the ranking official at Rheims, informed them that the introduction Pitt had scrambled to find came from a Monsieur Coustier, a shopkeeper who could get them into the local wholesalers, but not much more. The abbé took the three young men under his wing. During their stay in Paris, they not only were able to spend time with the Marquis de Lafayette but were also able to meet Benjamin Franklin and even spend time with the French royal family, including Queen Marie Antoinette, who had heard of their difficulty in obtaining a viable introduction.

"I've been curious to meet you three young Englishmen," the queen remarked. "What is this I hear about your excellent connections here in France? Is it true that you actually had a letter from a neighborhood grocer?" She paused long enough to make Pitt, Wilberforce, and Eliot suffer in embarrassment for their faux pas. "Do not worry, my young friends. You are most welcome in our country. We will show you we are not quite the barbarians you think we are."

four

Wilberforce was delighted when the word went out that the king might soon appoint William Pitt prime minister. He believed Pitt was deserving of the honor, and although he would be the youngest prime minister ever, he certainly would not be the least qualified. Many in Commons agreed with Wilberforce's opinion and promised their support. Pitt would need all the friends he could find. Wilberforce was a gifted speaker, and every ounce of his wit would be needed to carry the day on some of the close votes to come. Pitt also needed trusted friends like Wilberforce for consultation and strategizing.

Wilberforce had no major goals of his own in Parliament, other than representing Hull well. He valued Pitt's friendship and supported his goals for reform in Parliament. He also shared Pitt's distaste for the way the war in America was handled. He expected no rewards from Pitt for his support, apart from his respect and loyalty. Some day he might aspire to a stronger seat in the House and set about to address some major issues, but for now, he was content to be Pitt's friend.

Pitt's rise to the highest office in the Parliament at such a young age was an amazing thing, and to be so close to a man with such potential gave Wilberforce great pleasure. But as he bumped along on the road to York, he thought about how Pitt might be helpful to him in the future. He probably could ask for some sort of position in the new government, since he would be one of Pitt's backers, and Pitt would probably win the election. Wilberforce knew he would not be given one of the major ministry posts, since he represented a relatively minor borough. And he didn't really want to be given an appointment, in any case. There seemed to be something more important in his future, though he didn't know what.

He thought about the gathering he would be attending and how it might fit into his own political future. He knew little about the meeting that had been called by the Yorkshire Association, a reform group formed a few years before. He had a slight acquaintance with the head of this group, Christopher Wyvill, a clergyman with an estate and some political influence. Wilberforce knew that the Yorkshire Association hoped to gain support at the meeting for sending a message to the king asking for a new election. These reformers would give their support to the reform goals of William Pitt and hoped that the meeting would help identify potential members of Parliament from Yorkshire who would back Pitt and his reform agenda.

Apart from giving support to his friend William Pitt at the coming political rally in York, young Wilberforce began thinking about a way he could help Pitt even more than by continuing to represent Hull. Wouldn't it be good for Pitt and for himself, as well, if he were to come away from the York meeting as one of the two candidates from Yorkshire in the next elections?

Wilberforce had shown above-average skill at the gambling tables that were common pastimes for those of his position, but the odds of going from an obscure M.P. from Hull to one of the two members from Yorkshire made him almost laugh out loud. It was not a new idea to him, but he hadn't even had the courage to mention it to his friend Pitt. There were twenty thousand electors in Yorkshire, almost twenty times the number of voters in Hull. In fact, these two Yorkshire seats had more constituent power than any others in the House of Commons.

In Hull, Wilberforce had benefitted from the name recognition of his wealthy merchant family, but in Yorkshire there was strong preference for those among the landed aristocracy over those from the business community. There were growing industrial cities such as Sheffield, Leeds, Halifax, and Bradford in Yorkshire, but those involved in industry were no match politically for the landed class. Land and titles were of far greater consequence in the British caste structure of the eighteenth century than the "new wealth" of the merchant class.

Wilberforce knew that he could not repeat the tactics that had gained him a seat in Hull. There he followed the common practice of providing payments to those who supported him. There he could travel about the entire borough, talking with electors and winning their confidence. Yorkshire was far too large to meet all the voters, and there was very little time before the election. The cost of providing payments averaging eight pounds per voter would be far more than he had.

In fact, elections had rarely been held in Yorkshire in the eighteenth century. Because it would have been so difficult and costly to campaign in the county, the backers of particular candidates organized "canvasses," systematically making contact with voters in various areas. These canvasses were the equivalent of modern opinion polls and were just as accurate. Within weeks, the backers of candidates could gather evidence of the amount of support their candidates had and, if successful, convince opponents that it would be futile to ask for an election.

As his carriage took him closer to York for the political rally, Wilberforce weighed the practicality of becoming a candidate from Yorkshire. A long shot? Indeed, it was like betting on a horse that had come in last ten races in a row. He was little known in the county and was from the wrong social and economic class. Moreover, there were two incumbents from the county fully intending to win out in the canvassing process. Francis Foljambe, one of the incumbents, was the nephew of Sir George Savile, who had held the seat for more than twenty years. Foljambe had the backing of both the Yorkshire Association and the powerful landed families. Yorkshire's other member, Henry Duncombe, had gained his seat in 1780 through the specific efforts of the Association members, so there was not much opportunity for Wilberforce to present himself as a preferred choice of the sponsors of the meeting in York, the Yorkshire Association.

"Welcome, Wilberforce," said William Mason, his host in York. Mason was from Hull and had agreed to host Wilberforce during the political meeting there.

"Thank you for agreeing to host me," Wilberforce replied. "Could you give me a bit of a briefing on the alignment of political forces at tomorrow's meeting? We who spend most of our time in London don't hear much about political events in places like Yorkshire."

"Of course, William. Better yet, the Association's head, Christopher Wyvill, is to be our guest for high tea, and he can give you a better explanation than I can. But let me give you a bit of information."

The main question was whether the voters at the meeting would support a request to the king to dissolve Parliament and call an election. The even more important issues were who would gain support as new members and how they would align on their backing of Charles Fox and the coalition on the one hand and William Pitt and his new government on the other hand. Mason was a backer of Pitt, which meant he would support Duncombe's reelection. Duncombe was resolute in his stand for reform and had the solid backing of the Yorkshire Association. Foljambe, on the other hand, was officially in support of reform, but he made no secret of his preference for Fox, as did his major backers, Lord Fitzwilliam and the most powerful landed families.

"Mason, I agree with everything you've said so far. I've supported Pitt in these last few months in the Commons. I've known him since our days at Cambridge, and I have the highest regard for his ability and his integrity. In fact, I came here specifically to do what I could to support efforts that might gain him backing from Yorkshire in forming a new government.

"If you don't mind my saying so, Mason, the weather here in York is horrible. How do you expect a decent showing at the meeting tomorrow? It's to be held outdoors on the castle grounds, yes? I'd be shocked if we get more than a handful of voters."

"Oh, they will come, Wilberforce. I've seen the carriages coming to town for several days, and most of the inns are full. You've heard the phrase 'idle rich,' right? What better do the leaders of the county have to do in March than to see their friends and choose sides in a major political fight? The speeches will be boring, of course, but there's a lot at stake. You'll be amazed when you see the crowd tomorrow. I'll wager that it will be in the thousands."

Mason's prediction was on the mark. Four thousand voters assembled on the castle grounds on March 25, in spite of weather that combined cold wind, hail, and rain. There was a covered platform for the speakers, but the crowd had to endure the bitterness of the weather without protection. Speaker after speaker held forth, expressing their support or opposition to William Pitt's plans for a new reform government. Duncombe spoke in support of Pitt, while his fellow incumbent, Francis Foljambe, declined to speak, sensing the crowd would not be friendly to his pro-Fox sentiments.

As head of the sponsoring group, Christopher Wyvill controlled access to the platform. The previous evening at William Mason's house, he had gratefully accepted the help of William Wilberforce in preparing his remarks for the day. Seeing Wilberforce near the platform in midafternoon,

Wyvill beckoned to him and offered him a place in the roster of speakers. He warned Wilberforce that the crowd was tired and cold and suggested he make it short and forceful and be sure he could be heard over the wind.

While waiting for his turn on the platform, Wilberforce wondered if he should have accepted Wyvill's invitation to speak. Who was he to try making an impression among this array of impressive speakers? What could he say that hadn't already been said? What hope did he have that the crowd wouldn't all head immediately to tea when he took the stand?

"Mr. Wilberforce made a most argumentative and eloquent speech, which was listened to with the most eager attention, and received with the loudest acclamations of applause," said the newspaper report of William's speech. "There was such an exquisite choice of expression, and pronounced with such rapidity, that we are unable to do it justice in any account we can give of it," continued the story.

Wilberforce used his knowledge of the India Bill to attack its sponsors, headed by Charles Fox, and to support its opponents, led by William Pitt. He cautioned the powerful landholders in the crowd that legislation like the India Bill could lead to future actions undermining their freedoms. James Boswell, the Scottish biographer of Samuel Johnson, said that he first thought he was listening to a shrimp of a man, but soon concluded that this was no shrimp, but a whale.[1]

The speech might have ended and the rally concluded with no direct benefit to Wilberforce had it not been for a helpful coincidence. After speaking for about an hour and realizing he needed to conclude very soon, Wilberforce saw a rustle of activity on the edge of the crowd. Was it a group of people getting ready to leave? No, it was a rider in a great hurry. As the man made his way through the crowd, it was apparent from his appearance he was a messenger from the king. Accurately guessing the content of the message, Wilberforce beckoned the man forward and read the message to the crowd. The note was from Pitt and addressed to Wilberforce, dated at noon the day before. It reported that Parliament had been dissolved. Wilberforce was a master of extemporaneous speaking, and he used the opportunity to declare that the immediate goals of the day's gathering had been reached, but the long-range goals would only be achieved if those present would declare their firm support for William Pitt in the coming election.

Wilberforce's speech did much for Pitt's cause, but it did even more to further Wilberforce's own ambitions. In his note, Pitt urged Wilberforce to do his best to gain support for their mutual reform goals, a tacit endorsement for Wilberforce, who Pitt could not have known would be on the platform at the time. Some members of the crowd got the point and called out that they wanted Wilberforce as one of their county's members. This must have seemed ludicrous to those who had never heard of the man an hour before, but all were impressed with him and only the Fox supporters were brave enough to question the idea of Wilberforce as a county candidate. The meeting ended with an endorsement of the king's action in dissolving Parliament but no agreement on how the voters would proceed to select their two members.

Supporters of Fox and Pitt selected different places to caucus over dinner and drinks. The Pitt people gathered at

York Tavern, but it turned out that support for Pitt was one of the few things on which the caucus could agree. They had many arguments during the evening, and heavy drinking added to the ill will. Wilberforce used the support he had gained that afternoon to assist Wyvill in making peace among the angry factions at the dinner. For his efforts, he gained the acclamation of some of the Pitt supporters for his candidacy as one of Yorkshire's members. As the meeting broke up, supporters of Wilberforce cried out that they would support his candidacy.

The next day, another gathering of Pitt supporters agreed to back Duncombe and Wilberforce as their candidates, rejecting a proposal from the Fox group that Duncombe and Foljambe be retained in office. Knowing that even a canvass would be expensive, and the cost of an election would be prohibitive, Pitt and Wilberforce supporters pledged ten thousand pounds to pursue the campaign. With growing support but no guarantee of the outcome, Wilberforce had to go back to Hull to campaign for his present seat. He accomplished that successfully, in spite of some resentment over his effort to gain the more prestigious position representing Yorkshire.

In less than two weeks from the rally in York, Wilberforce not only won the Hull seat as a backup, but participated energetically in the canvassing of Yorkshire. Wyvill was able to mobilize a network of local Yorkshire Association committees on behalf of the Duncombe/ Wilberforce ticket. The canvass showed the two Pitt candidates had four times the support of the Fox candidates, Foljambe and William Weddell. The rest was anticlimactic. The Fox backers withdrew, one of their leaders grumbling about their defeat by ragamuffins like Wilberforce who were not part of the aristocracy.

Wilberforce's cryptic diary entry understated his amazement and happiness at his surprising victory. He wrote, "Up early—breakfasted tavern—rode frisky horse to castle—elected—chaired—dined York Tavern." His friend William Pitt understood the significance of the victory and its implications for both of them. Pitt wrote, "I can never enough congratulate you on such a glorious success."[2] In a few days' time, Wilberforce had gone from a relatively weak position in Parliament to one of its most powerful seats and thus had created a base from which he might undertake almost any cause in the future.

five

M ilner, I can't thank you enough for joining us on the trip to France," Wilberforce said with relief. He would have preferred to vacation in England, but his mother, his sister Sally, and two female cousins were determined to visit France, and he was stuck with accompanying them.

"Wilberforce, how could I argue with the chance to get away from Cambridge and share the company of such a bright and pleasant individual as you? I suppose you needed an excuse not to ride in the carriage with the women, correct?"

"Yes, of course. But you won't quote me on that, will you?"

Wilberforce had had some difficulty finding a friend to join him on the trip to and from France. A fortunate meeting with Milner in Scarborough had prompted him to invite the professor to join the expedition. At least they could talk about their days at Hull School and Cambridge, where Milner had led the class in mathematics. Wilberforce knew there was a lot he could learn from Milner. He was a little bothered by the fact that Milner's brother Joseph had become an evangelical, but Milner assured him he was not about to try to convert anyone.

Wilberforce himself found the preaching of Theophilius Lindsey quite interesting. This impressive thinker and speaker had concluded that much of the New Testament material was added by early followers of Christ, who made Him into the sort of divine being He never presented Himself to be. He said the stories of the miracles and the healings, even the resurrection story, were add-ons from people who got carried away with their admiration for Christ. Lindsey believed in God and the Scripture but concentrated on the parts of the Bible that were most consistent with the reasoning of modern man. He called himself a Unitarian, based on the understanding that God is one being, not three separate persons.

Milner had heard about Lindsey but wouldn't go far out of his way to hear him preach, as he told Wilberforce. Milner believed the Bible is God's inspired and authoritative message to us. Some parts of it he could not explain completely, but simply because he couldn't understand something in the Bible didn't make it untrue. He admitted that there was much in his life that didn't square with the evangelical life, but where it matters most—in his understanding of and commitment to Jesus as Savior and Lord of his life—he could be called an evangelical. The two agreed to disagree, spending their time discussing other matters.

After the party had spent some weeks in France, Pitt wrote to Wilberforce, urging him to return for the introduction of a parliamentary reform bill. Wilberforce, who had no great love for French food and culture, was happy for an excuse to return. Before departing, he noticed a book owned by his cousin Bessy Smith—Philip Doddridge's *Rise and Progress of Religion in the Soul.* Doddridge, who had died several decades before, was something of a spiritual father to Whitefield and Wesley in his emphasis on salvation by faith in Christ. The book was well written and standard fare among Christians of the day. Wondering if the book would help pass the long hours on the trip back to England, Wilberforce asked Milner if it would be worth reading. Milner knew the book and endorsed it enthusiastically. He suggested they read and discuss it together on their return trip.

Doddridge's views didn't square very well with those of the Reverend Lindsey, and Wilberforce wasn't sure whom he found more believable. Doddridge wouldn't fare too well in the theology debates at Cambridge, but there was something about the directness of his reasoning that Wilberforce rather liked. Lindsey had a way of picking and choosing parts of the Bible that suited him, content to set aside any part that couldn't be worked out through human reasoning. "It's sort of like worshiping part of God and ignoring the other parts of Him, don't you think?" he asked Milner.

"I think we must accept by faith the key elements of the gospel, such as the divinity of Jesus, the inspiration of the Scriptures, Christ's resurrection, and the need for repentance and conversion," Milner responded. "Do I understand all of that? No, but I believe it. And I trust a loving God to reveal as much of the truth of the gospel as is important for us to understand."

When the time came to collect the ladies and escort them home, Milner agreed to join Wilberforce again. Wilberforce had been busy in the meantime. There was plenty of work for him to do in Commons, and keeping his constituents happy had been exhausting. He and Pitt had written and introduced a new bill on parliamentary reform, but it would be another matter to get it approved. The bill would eliminate thirty-five of the many "rotten" boroughs, but those who had profited from the system were understandably upset.

Pitt was in an awkward spot. He was the number-one champion of reform in the country, but he had entered Parliament from a rotten borough himself after losing his campaign in Cambridge.

Since he and Milner had returned to London, Wilberforce had attended most of the sessions of Commons, but that didn't keep him from spending time talking with his friends, singing, drinking, and dancing. His frail body was not up to that sort of life anymore, and he needed a holiday after only four months back at work.

"William, we've hardly seen you during this trip," Wilberforce's mother complained. "What on earth do you talk about with Isaac Milner for hour after hour? Can't you spend a little time with us?"

"I'm sorry, Mother. I must say I'm rather surprised at myself. Believe it or not, I hunted up my copy of the Greek New Testament before this trip, and we have been reading it along the way, talking about some of the difficult passages."

46

"Oh, William. You've been so fortunate to be elected to one of the most important positions in the Parliament. You know very well that religious fanaticism will not be acceptable to your constituents. You also know that many of the Methodists completely cut themselves off from the life of our social groups. They don't go to the opera and theater and don't dine out very often. You could throw away your entire career and all the good things you might do if you choose to pursue views that don't seem to fit at all with the teaching of the Church of England."

"Mother, I love you and my sister very much, but whatever I do with all these things is now my business, not yours. My views on religion haven't affected my daily life much at all. No one in politics would have any reason to call me a religious fanatic. Now I can only say I think I believe in Christ as my Savior and Lord. I don't think my obedience to Christ will take me away from the Church of England. It may take me back to the most important things at the heart of the church."

The changes in Wilberforce's inner life had been steady and dramatic, and soon the inner changes began to affect his outward life. While still in Europe with his family, he took some small but significant steps toward what he felt was a more godly style of living. He began to abstain from some activities on Sundays, such as attending the opera and theater. He then began to arise early each day for prayer and meditation and soon after that began a daily spiritual journal. Those times of personal reflection led to enormous inner turmoil before he reached a point of spiritual equilibrium. He later recalled,

*As soon as I reflected seriously, the deep guilt
and black ingratitude of my past life forced itself
on me in the strongest colors, and I condemned
myself for having wasted precious time, and
opportunities and talents. . . . It was not so much
the fear of punishment by which I was affected, as
a sense of my great sinfulness in having so long
neglected the unspeakable mercies of my God and
Savior; and such was the effect which this thought
produced, that for months I was in a state of the
deepest depression, from strong convictions of my
guilt. Indeed nothing which I have ever read in the
accounts of others exceeded what I then felt.*[1]

Actually, he was going through a period of spiritual
struggle that is much more common than he thought, particularly among those like himself who had established their
lives as an adult and a professional and then found themselves questioning all their assumptions and goals.

six

Central to William Wilberforce's spiritual struggle in late 1785 was a question that has been faced by many who have determined to submit to the lordship of Christ. Those who have come to a fresh new relationship with Christ as adults have often wondered if turning away from many of their worldly habits and activities would necessitate leaving their career, as well. To surrender to Christ as Savior and Lord means being obedient to the Holy Spirit's leadings that might take one into a new career and possibly away from the friendships that have been important in one's life.

William sat at his desk, struggling with the wording of his letter to one of his closest friends, the prime minister of England, William Pitt. The two had spent a great deal of time together socially and in political strategizing.

Wilberforce's association with Pitt had been crucial in his election as a member from Yorkshire. In turn, Wilberforce's efforts to promote Pitt's causes in that election had been central to solidifying Pitt's political base in Parliament. They had much in common from their time together at Cambridge. Pitt was the more studious of the two at the university and the more serious of the two in seeking and holding leadership at the national level.

As he thought about what to say to Pitt, Wilberforce looked at some of the entries in his journal. They revealed the intensity of his new spiritual commitment and the turmoil he felt about what this might mean in his life, personally and politically:

> *I must awake to my dangerous state, and never be at rest till I have made peace with God. My heart is so hard, my blindness so great, that I cannot get a due hatred of sin, though I see I am all corrupt, and blinded to the perception of spiritual things. True, Lord, I am wretched, and miserable, and blind, and naked. What infinite love, that Christ should die to save such a sinner, and how necessary is it He should save us altogether, that we may appear before God with nothing of our own!*
>
> *Pride is my greatest stumbling block; and there is danger in it in two ways—lest it should make me desist from a Christian life, through fear of the world, my friends, etc.; or if I persevere, lest it should make me vain of so doing.*
>
> *O God, give me a heart of flesh! Nothing so convinces me of the dreadful state of my own mind,*

*as the possibility, which, if I did not know it from
experience, I should believe impossible, of my
being ashamed of Christ. Ashamed of the creator
of all things! One who has received infinite pardon
and mercy, ashamed of the dispenser of it, and that
in a country where His name is professed! Oh,
what should I have done in persecuting times?[1]*

Having reread the journal entries, Wilberforce thought about the time that week he had been with Pitt. He felt ashamed he had not talked with Pitt about his new faith in Christ but felt he must not wait for the perfect chance to talk. At the time, letters were the favored means of expressing deeply personal issues, so it's not surprising that a letter would be the first means of telling Pitt about his spiritual renewal.

Wilberforce agonized over the wording of his letter to Pitt, for in it he was expressing the possibility that he might have to leave behind his promising career in politics, if this is what was required of him to be faithful in following Christ. Whether or not he would drop out of politics, at the very least he would leave behind many aspects of the social life that had been central to who he had been from his university days. He also told Pitt he would no longer be a "party man" in a different sense. If he were to stay in politics, he felt he would no longer be free to support his allies and friends in Parliament at all times but would find it necessary to follow his own moral and spiritual convictions, whatever those might be. Wilberforce ended the letter by expressing the hope that their friendship might remain intact, even though they might have to relate to one another differently. Rather than risk that their differences in moral and spiritual values might sever their friendship, Wilberforce asked that they not even talk of these matters further.

The reply from Prime Minister Pitt arrived very quickly, and Wilberforce read it with some anxiety. "You will not suspect me of thinking lightly of any moral or religious motives which guide you. But forgive me if I cannot help expressing my fear that you are deluding yourself into principles which have but too much tendency to counteract your own object, and to render your virtues and your talents useless both to yourself and to mankind." Pitt went on to directly challenge Wilberforce's thinking that faithfulness to Christ might require him to leave his career in politics. "If a Christian may act in the several relations of life, must he seclude himself from all to become so? Surely the principles as well as the practice of Christianity are simple, and lead not to meditation only, but to action."

Wilberforce had suggested that the two might no longer be close friends if their values were substantially different. Pitt questioned the need for Wilberforce's spiritual zeal to create a rift between them:

> As to any public conduct which your opinion
> may ever lead you to, I will not disguise to you that
> few things could go nearer my heart than to find
> myself differing from you on any great principle. I
> trust and believe that it is a circumstance that can
> hardly occur. . .believe me it is impossible that it
> should shake the sentiments of affection and friend-
> ship which I bear towards you, and which I must be
> forgetful and insensible indeed if I ever could part

with. They are sentiments engraved on my heart,
and will never be effaced or weakened. . . .[2]

Not content to let an exchange of letters be the end of this discussion, Prime Minister Pitt went out of his way the following day to call on Wilberforce at Wimbledon. The discussion was long and intense. Pitt assured Wilberforce that their friendship was too important to both of them to be threatened by their differing views of religion.

Pitt considered himself a Christian and a faithful member of the church. He admired Wilberforce's courage in putting his faith ahead of everything else but begged him not to throw away all he could accomplish in his life through politics. Pitt was sure that one of these days Wilberforce would find a cause that would ignite his talents and energies. "Can you not serve your God while in politics, instead of heading off into some sort of monastic life?" he exclaimed.

Wilberforce replied that perhaps God would open a way for him to stay in public life while still being obedient to His directions, but either way, he had to be faithful to God's leading.

Pitt was not ready to follow Wilberforce's spiritual leadership, but he hoped that he could count on his friend to keep his seat from Yorkshire and back his causes in the House whenever he could. He would try to understand if Wilberforce felt he must oppose him on some points and asked that Wilberforce respect him when he took a position that Wilberforce could not support.

"Amazing grace! How sweet the sound, that saved a wretch

like me! I once was lost, but now am found, was blind but now I see."

The words of that hymn may well have been going through his mind as Wilberforce walked around the block where the hymn's author, John Newton, lived. The entries in Wilberforce's journal at the time expressed many of the same sentiments as the hymn: the great joy in deliverance from spiritual blindness and wretchedness. This was the same John Newton whom Wilberforce had heard preach in boyhood and who was part of the spiritual environment from which his mother had abruptly removed him. And this was the same John Newton who had been delivered from his own lifestyle as a sea captain and the institutional evil in which he had participated for years—the slave trade. Newton had since responded to a call to the ministry in the Church of England. His sentiments were very much with the growing evangelical movement inside and outside the church.

"It makes the wounded spirit whole, and calms the troubled breast;'Tis manna to the hungry soul, and to the weary, rest; and to the weary, rest." These lines from another of Newton's hymns, "How Sweet the Name of Jesus Sounds," may also have been running through William's mind as he went around the block a second time at Newton's parish, St. Mary Woolnoth. Certainly he was ready for some rest from his struggles to be faithful to the leading of the Holy Spirit. The letter to William Pitt and subsequent conversation had brought some emotional relief to Wilberforce, but he couldn't get away from the sense that he was supposed to go see John Newton. In his journal he had argued with himself about it. He knew it would be helpful to establish contact with the pastor whose sermons he had valued as a boy. Could it be that Pitt was selfishly urging him to stay in politics? Could it be that someone like Newton, without a vested interest in politics, would counsel Wilberforce to make a clean break from his present life and follow God's leading into some very different direction?

In his journal, Wilberforce had correctly named the source of his hesitation about meeting with Newton. It was spiritual pride that was stopping Wilberforce from going ahead to meet Newton, a lowly preacher, far below Wilberforce in social standing. More to the point, Newton was one of the despised "Methodists," those who had experienced the kind of conversion that was emphasized so much by John Wesley and the other evangelicals. There was no Methodist denomination at the time, but those who believed in and practiced the emphasis on conversion and forgiveness from sins were all labeled as Methodists and were viewed with derision, reflecting the sentiments of Wilberforce's mother when she had brought him home from her brother-in-law's custody.

Wilberforce had approached William Pitt about his new spiritual experience with little hesitation. With Newton it was a different matter. Wilberforce went to find Newton's house but at first lacked the courage to talk with him. Instead, he wrote a letter to Newton proposing that they meet but was so paranoid about someone learning of their contact that he tore the signature from the letter and urged Newton not to tell anyone they had been in touch.

William knew his Bible well and might have thought about the Old Testament account of Naaman, an army commander who was directed by the prophet Elisha to wash in the Jordan River in order to receive God's healing from leprosy. What could be simpler? But from Naaman's point of view, what could be more humiliating than to wash in the Jordan, not nearly as impressive as the rivers back in Naaman's home in Damascus? For Wilberforce, going to visit John Newton was like washing in the Jordan River. It meant humbling himself and taking the risk of being identified with one of the better-known evangelical clergymen of the day.

At last, Wilberforce's determination to follow Christ at any cost won out over his fear and pride, and he kept his appointment with Newton. One of Wilberforce's fears was that Newton's counsel would be different from Pitt's, that Wilberforce needed to leave his career in politics to be completely obedient to Christ. Newton himself had left his work as a ship captain after his conversion. But this was not the counsel Newton gave Wilberforce. "The Lord has raised you up for the good of His church and for the good of His nation," declared Newton, echoing the point made a few days before by Pitt.

"The very fact of your being obedient today is probably of more consequence than anything that has transpired today," Newton said. He believed Wilberforce had much to offer the work of God's kingdom. He didn't want Wilberforce to do anything but follow God's leading, whether that meant staying in Parliament or leaving. That said, Newton believed God had some great work ahead for Wilberforce.

seven

"The first years I was in Parliament, I did nothing—nothing that is to any purpose. My own distinction was my darling object." This was the way William Wilberforce assessed his first two years representing Yorkshire in Parliament. Was he too hard on himself? Yes, but at the time he was introspective and unhappy, feeling that there was some higher purpose for his life now that he had fully surrendered to Christ.

It was true that Wilberforce did not accomplish much of lasting consequence in public life in 1786 and 1787, other than becoming familiar with the procedures and the culture of the House of Commons. One of his first initiatives had a noble aim—parliamentary reform. But after Wilberforce became more familiar with the particular bill he had supported, he was relieved that it failed to pass the

House of Lords. The bill would have required voter registration to occur in one place and on one day in the member's district. On further reflection, it appeared that this restriction would hinder voter participation, particularly in a large jurisdiction like Yorkshire.[1]

Wilberforce's other early attempt at legislative work also failed and helped him realize that public policy issues were far more complex than they first appeared. Again, the cause was noble—reform of the criminal justice system. But the remedy proved to be problematic. Parliamentary measures in that day were wordy and obtuse, at least for modern tastes. Wilberforce's bill was entitled, "A Bill for Regulating the Disposal after Execution of the Bodies of Criminals Executed for Certain Offences, and for Changing the Sentence Pronounced upon Female Convicts in Certain Cases of High and Petty Treason."[2]

Wilberforce's bill would have outlawed a practice he and his supporters considered to be brutal and inappropriate—the burning or dissection of the bodies of convicted criminals once they were hanged. Opponents of his measure saw the practice as a deterrent against crime, but Wilberforce despised such spectacles. One hanging and burning that year had attracted twenty thousand spectators to Newgate prison. But banning dissection of these bodies would have had the unintended effect of hindering scientific research and medical training, leaving it to body snatchers to provide cadavers for these legitimate purposes. In any event, the House of Lords defeated the bill, its spokesman calling it "ill-advised and impracticable."

Wilberforce struggled to find a comfortable place for himself socially as well as politically, in view of his new spiritual commitments. He continued to withdraw from many of his previous social involvements, feeling they were contrary to his convictions as a serious follower of Christ. He resigned from a number of the social clubs in which he had been active and which were considered to be both the privilege and the duty of members of Parliament. He stopped gambling, which had been a centerpiece of his socializing earlier, and stopped going to dances and the theater.

As a politician of growing prominence, Wilberforce was expected to appear at major events in the county he represented, such as horse races, balls, and dinners. While knowing his absence from these events might hurt him politically, he no longer enjoyed the frivolity of upper-class social life. Typical of the uncertainty he felt about the social choices he was making was his comment to his political ally Christopher Wyvill that his constituents might misunderstand his lack of participation in social events. He wondered if his behavior would "excite disgust rather than cordiality." Wyvill encouraged him to chart his own course rather than violate his convictions and priorities.[3]

In place of the social whirl that had filled Wilberforce's younger years, he set about to make up for his lack of diligence in his studies at Cambridge. During an extended stay with friends near Nottingham, he maintained a daily routine that included up to ten hours a day of studying history, economics, literature, philosophy, and science. He limited his social time with his hosts and their guests so he could spend ample time with the ideas of the great thinkers he had neglected at the university: Montesquieu, Adam Smith,

Blackstone, Locke, Pope, Johnson. At the same time, Wilberforce included careful study of the Bible among his new disciplines. His cousin Henry Thornton said of the "new Wilberforce" at this time, "his enlarged mind, his affectionate and understanding manners, and his very superior piety were exactly calculated to supply what was wanting to my improvement and my establishment in the right course."[4]

The changes in Wilberforce's life during 1786, as he engaged in serious study and reduced his social activities, prepared him to give greater attention to his purpose in life. He had been completely unsure where he should devote his energies in the Parliament. Though he had decided that God would have him continue to pursue politics as a vocation, he did not know whether there was some particular moral or spiritual cause he should pursue. During this time of seeking direction, seeds began to be planted in the mind and heart of Wilberforce for what would become his best-known life accomplishment, the abolition of the slave trade.

The Portuguese first transported slaves to Europe for sale in 1444. For fifty years, the slaves were put to work only in Portugal, and the volume of the trade was modest. The Portuguese first took slaves to the New World colonies in 1503 and in a few years began direct shipment from Africa to America. English traders did not participate in the early years of this trade, and English opinion did not favor this type of trade. But when England began to acquire colonies in the Caribbean and North America, slaves became a solution for the needed manual labor of plantation agriculture. Moreover, English merchants and shippers began to see the potential for major profits in the three-way trade of goods of interest to slave traders in Africa, the shipping and sale of the slaves to the New World, and the return of produce and precious metals to England and Europe. The attractive profits overpowered the lingering moral concerns about the slave trade and slavery itself, at least for most people.

By the time Wilberforce became involved in politics, England was in the business of transporting slaves to the New World. Some merchants and shippers were becoming very wealthy from the trade. There had actually been a judicial ruling in 1772 that declared slavery inconsistent with English law. The abolitionist Granville Sharp had brought a case to Chief Justice Mansfield, demanding that James Somerset, a slave in Jamaica, be freed. This provided a legal precedent for ending slavery, but it had done nothing to end the slave trade.

Was it a coincidence that Wilberforce came into regular contact with the small group of abolitionists in England? Was it coincidental that at this time he was casting about for some worthy purpose for his efforts in public life? Was it also a coincidence that some of those who had taken up the slavery cause were persons Wilberforce highly regarded? The answer to all three questions is no, at least for those who believe in a sovereign God at work in the lives of believers who are determined to follow God's purpose in their lives. By mid-1786, Wilberforce was definitely such a person, and it is fascinating to trace the quiet steps by which he came into contact with the abolitionists and eventually became their most determined and successful worker, at least in public life.

One place to start the story of Wilberforce's "conversion"

to the cause of slavery is with Captain Sir Charles Middleton, Comptroller of the Navy and head of the Navy Board during and after the war with the American colonies. Middleton was also a member of Parliament and one of the few in that body who held to Wilberforce's strong evangelical convictions. A major influence in Middleton's spiritual development was his wife, Margaret, who was converted early in life under the ministry of George Whitefield. She was an artist, a musician, and intellectual. More to the point, she was a person motivated to help those in need. It was said of her that she was "constantly on the stretch in seeking out opportunities of promoting in every possible way the ease, the comfort, the prosperity, the happiness temporal and eternal, of all within her reach. . . ."[5]

One influence in the Middletons' concern about the suffering of slaves was their vicar at Teston Church, James Ramsay. The Reverend Ramsay had been the surgeon on a ship commanded by Middleton in 1759. Middleton had sent Ramsay to check on the conditions on a British ship carrying slaves, a ship the French had captured and Middleton and his crew reclaimed. Both Ramsay and Middleton were appalled at the condition of the slaves, who were suffering terribly from the plague. Subsequently, Ramsay had been rector and medical supervisor of plantations for the British colony of St. Kitts. He had seen the human suffering resulting from the slave trade and some of the evils of slavery itself. He served on St. Kitts for nineteen years, earning the disfavor of the plantation owners for his efforts to improve the slaves' conditions.

After moving to Teston, Ramsay reported to the Middletons about conditions among slaves in the Caribbean. With their encouragement, he published his "Essay on the Treatment and Conversion of Slaves in the British Sugar Colonies." His point about conversion was that the slaves would be unlikely to accept the gospel of Christ when nothing about their environment evidenced God's love at work among the whites. In response to a friendly reviewer who thought he had condoned the slave trade while condemning slavery, Ramsay wrote a second pamphlet about the "barbarous cruelty" and oppression of the slave trade itself.[6]

The number of Teston parish members concerned about slavery began to multiply. The Middletons invited Bishop Beilby Porteus of Chester (later bishop of London) to come to Teston to join in the discussions about slavery. Even more significantly, Vicar Ramsay invited a young clergyman, Thomas Clarkson, to spend some time at Teston to join in the dialogue. Ramsay had read Clarkson's pamphlet, "Essay on the Slavery and Commerce of the Human Species," which had won Clarkson a prize at Cambridge.

The Middletons and Ramsays were moved by the story Clarkson told at dinner one day about traveling to London after completing the essay:

> *I stopped my horse occasionally, and dismounted and walked. I frequently tried to persuade myself in these intervals that the contents of my essay could not be true. The more, however, I reflected upon them or rather upon the authorities on which they were founded, the more I gave them credit. Coming in sight of Wade's Mill in Hertfordshire, I sat down disconsolate on the turf by the roadside and held my horse. Here a thought came*

*into my mind—that, if the contents of the essay
were true, it was time some persons should see
these calamities to their end.*[7]

Clarkson's hosts at Teston could not have been more
impressed by his knowledge of the subject and his passion
to move from discussion into action. "Well, young man,"
said Middleton, "since your pamphlet does indeed contain
the truth, are you ready to step forward to be the one to
devote your life to ending slavery?"

"I am, indeed," responded Clarkson. "By God's grace I
will devote myself fully to this cause."[8]

The connections between the Teston group and William
Wilberforce are not apparent at first, but he met the
Middletons through their son-in-law and came to know Sir
Charles when he was elected to Parliament in 1784.
Wilberforce became a frequent guest at the Middleton home.

In the autumn of 1786, an important conversation
occurred at the Middleton home over the breakfast table.
The topic was the need for a champion of abolition in
Parliament. An obvious first choice was Middleton.
"Indeed, I think, Sir Charles," said his wife, "you ought to
bring the subject before the House, and demand a parliamentary enquiry in the nature of that hideous traffic, so dis-
graceful to the British character."[9]

Middleton agreed that someone needed to bring the situation to Parliament's attention but disagreed that he
should be the one to do so. He went on to explain his lia-
bilities. He had expertise with naval issues but not the
stature to provide leadership on broader issues. He was not
a great speaker, and he did not have a close relationship

with William Pitt, the prime minister.

"William Wilberforce is the one, my friends," said Middleton. "He comes from a much stronger district, and he's an excellent speaker. He's very close to Pitt. He has committed his life to Christ and would understand this is an issue directly related to his Christian values. And, unless I'm mistaken, I think he's casting about for just such a cause to which he could devote his political career."

Middleton was right about Wilberforce's readiness for such a cause. Middleton wrote to Wilberforce, asking him to bring this matter to the Parliament. Wilberforce replied that he agreed the issue was of great importance, but that he felt unequal to provide leadership to the cause in Parliament. In spite of his feeling of inadequacy, he accepted.[10]

Having made this tentative commitment, Wilberforce followed up with a series of meetings with Thomas Clarkson. Clarkson's pamphlet and subsequent research on the subject provided a body of facts and arguments on which Wilberforce could draw for the coming efforts in Parliament. The meetings in early 1787 were expanded to include others committed to the cause, including Middleton and Ramsay. Another participant was Granville Sharp, the abolition activist whose legal efforts in the Somerset Case of 1772 had laid a foundation for the case against slavery.

A dinner hosted by Clarkson in March 1787 was the first semipublic occasion at which Wilberforce agreed to bring the issue to Parliament. Two other members of the Commons were present at the dinner when Wilberforce was asked to declare his willingness to move forward as the principal sponsor of hearings and subsequent legislation. He had found one of the purposes in life he had been seeking. From that time forward, he never hesitated in giving of his energy and talent to the cause of the slaves.

The many discussions about the need to abolish slavery led to the formation in May 1787 of the Committee for the Abolition of the Slave Trade. Granville Sharp chaired the committee; Clarkson was a member and one of its hardest workers. Most of the members were Quakers, whose behind-the-scenes work for abolition had been going on for years. They drew part of their inspiration from the efforts of the American Quaker John Woolman. Wilberforce did not formally join the abolition committee but worked closely with it in the months and years to come.

One of the major strategic discussions between Wilberforce and the other abolitionists was whether it was wise to seek the immediate end of slavery or if their first goal should be only the ending of the trade in slaves. No one involved in this effort believed that it was sufficient to end the slave trade, but after vigorous discussion there was agreement that the trade would be the first target. A factor in the decision to proceed in stages toward the ultimate goal was a constitutional issue. Supporters of slavery could have argued that Parliament had no jurisdiction over private property, especially in the colonies, which were not formally a part of England. The pragmatists in this discussion successfully argued that no one could question the right of Parliament to regulate trade, so the abolition of the slave trade was an attainable goal.

Pitt, the master politician, was not deeply passionate about the slave issue, though he believed that slavery should eventually be ended. His advice on the issue to his friend

Wilberforce came from the perspective of a political tactician, not an ideologue. Waiting too long to take this stand could deprive Wilberforce of his single great issue in Parliament. Without such an issue, Pitt believed, Wilberforce would be forgotten a generation later. He was right that this could have happened, but Wilberforce did take up the leadership on the issue, and he certainly wasn't forgotten.

eight

M r. Wilberforce, it's a pleasure to see you again," said Thomas Clarkson. "I appreciate the commitment you've made to lead the cause against slavery in the Parliament."

The Committee for the Abolition of the Slave Trade, which Clarkson had been working with, wanted to end the slave trade as quickly as possible before tackling slavery itself. "Do you think we can expect to bring this to a speedy conclusion in the Parliament? The committee and I are willing to spare no effort toward that end."

"Clarkson, my friend," Wilberforce replied, "I would love to think that we might reach our first goal of eliminating the vile trade in the next year or so, but I have no way of knowing if that can be done. Quite honestly, we could have a very long battle ahead of us, especially to eliminate slavery itself."

"Well, Parliament is in recess now. What can be done before you proceed with a bill?"

Wilberforce believed Clarkson and the committee should spend every waking hour for the next few months gathering information on the evils of the trade. Third-hand reports and speculation about what might be occurring on the high seas would get them nowhere in the House of Commons; they needed indisputable, eyewitness evidence, willing and creditable people who would agree to testify. Someone had to witness how the slaves were captured, how they were loaded on the ships, and the kind of treatment they received while crossing the Atlantic. "We must have facts. We must have numbers. We must be able to show that the slave trade is a poor investment, since large numbers of the slaves die before they even reach the West Indies and America."

Clarkson was well qualified to do this research because of his previous study of slavery. "Set about your work as though you don't know a thing," Wilberforce urged. "Leave no stone unturned. I'll see that you are given access to the documents in the Custom House and elsewhere, but you can't limit your investigation to London. You must go to Bristol and the other ports where the ships are coming and going. You must find people willing to tell what they've seen in Africa, on the high seas, and in the colonies. With persuasion, some will be willing to testify in our hearings. Others won't, but you can use their evidence. Of course if you do your job well, your reputation will precede you, and the defenders of slavery will do all they can to hinder your work."

Clarkson first went to Bristol to begin gathering information, going about his work with all the diligence that Wilberforce and the abolition committee had hoped for and expected. Some of those he met were willing to cooperate fully, such as the retired surgeon Alexander Falconbridge, who had served on four slaving ships. Others were very cautious about talking to him for fear word would get back to their former or future employers in the trade. When Clarkson doubted the accuracy of some statements he received, he traced the reports to their source. For example, he measured a particular ship to confirm that it was designed to give each slave only three square feet of deck space. When he began to discover that the crew members of many slave ships were treated much worse than those on other ships, he tracked down the records of the ships to confirm the reports of large numbers of sailors' deaths.

Clarkson went from Bristol to Gloucester, Worcester, and Chester. Fortunately, Alexander Falconbridge was willing to go with Clarkson to provide some physical protection and help convince the skeptical that the information they were gathering was accurate. Clarkson gathered physical evidence related to the mistreatment of slaves, purchasing such things as shackles, thumbscrews, and other instruments of torture. He was able to collect information from literally thousands of seamen and the cargo they carried. He returned to London with a large supply of evidence, a deep sadness about the inhumanity revealed by his sources, and a determination that there would be no turning back in the abolition movement.[1]

Wilberforce gave notice of his intentions when Commons was back in session.

Mr. Speaker, I rise to give notice that in the next session I will be ready to offer my bill that would bring an end to the slave trade. We have just celebrated the birth of our Savior, Jesus, and I can think of no better time than this to extend the compassion of our Lord to the suffering of hundreds of thousands of our brethren from the continent of Africa. I will not go into our case today, but suffice it to say that the weight of evidence on the side of abolishing this horrible trade is very convincing. I shall be most happy to pass along some of this evidence to my esteemed colleagues in anticipation of our debate and action in the future.

"Mr. Speaker, I rise in support of the honorable gentleman from Yorkshire," said Charles James Fox, who had served in Parliament for twenty years.

I must confess that I had intended to take the first step in this noble cause before it was brought by my friend, Mr. Wilberforce. I do not resent for a minute that he has taken the first step. I trust and believe we will come to see the merits of this case and will end the brutality that has sullied the reputation of our empire. Please join me in welcoming this effort on behalf of England and the people of Africa.

It may have been the goodwill of the holiday season and the favorable response he received when he announced the plans for a slave trade bill that gave Wilberforce the feeling that abolition was on its way toward speedy success. It also may have been the support he knew he had from Prime Minister William Pitt, as well as the mountain of evidence gathered by Thomas Clarkson. Indeed, things looked very good for the cause of abolition in February 1788. King George III directed that a Privy Council committee begin an investigation of the slave trade. Thomas Clarkson's hard work began to pay off as these hearings made available the first widespread knowledge about the brutalities of the slave trade and slavery.

But the optimism of Wilberforce and the abolitionists in early 1788 was premature. The Privy Council not only provided the public with knowledge of the abolitionists' case, but it gave the opponents of abolition a chance to develop their rebuttal. Far from being victims, the slave interests argued, the slaves were being rescued from death for their crimes or from abuse or death as prisoners of war. Witnesses asserted that they had seen the jubilation of slaves on their way to a better life in the New World.

Meanwhile, some of those who had given information to Clarkson about the slave trade had decided that it would be too risky to testify. In fact, one of Clarkson's possible witnesses had apparently been deceptive when the two of them had met in Bristol; he showed up to testify for the defenders of the slave trade.

Wilberforce had not only underestimated the strength of the opposition witnesses but had also failed to assess the strength of the opposition within the government. His friend William Pitt knew that the king and the other members of the royal family, along with most of the Cabinet, were firmly on the proslave-trade side of the battle. Pitt was in a position to predict where the members of Parliament would take their stand on the slave trade. Sizable numbers were committed to defend the interests of the ship owners, the investors involved in shipping, and those involved in the economy of the New World. Substantial numbers of members were more concerned about freedom of trade and personal property than about the slave economy itself. They shared the sentiments of English naval hero Admiral Lord Nelson, who said he would use all the energy he had to defend the status quo in the West Indian colonies "against the damnable doctrine of Wilberforce and his hypocritical allies."[2]

In February 1788, just as the Privy Council hearings were getting underway, and Wilberforce was hard at work on the presentation he would make introducing the bill in the Commons, he became severely ill. He had never been particularly strong physically, but this illness was far more serious than anything he had experienced before. He had a high fever, chronic exhaustion, and severe digestive problems. Doctors knew little about his disorders at the time, but today we would call it ulcerative colitis, partially caused by stress. Had he not submitted to medical care and taken a break from his duties in Parliament, he might have died before reaching his thirtieth birthday.

"My dear friend Mr. Pitt," Wilberforce wrote from Bath in early April 1788, where he was being treated and getting rest.

You know of my great affection and respect for you and that I would never call on you for help unless it were absolutely necessary. I am beginning

*to feel a little better from the treatments I am
receiving here, but my doctors and my family
members have forbidden me from returning to
London for this session. You know that the supporters of the slave trade have presented a very
vigorous case in the Privy Council hearings. We
can't let their voices go unchallenged and must
set things in motion for a debate in the Commons,
where we will be able to answer the many ridiculous statements given in the committee sessions.
Before I came to Bath, we talked about the possibility that I might need to prevail on you to introduce the motion in the House, and now I must ask
you to do exactly that. I know you have far too
much to handle on other fronts, but the bill must
be brought forward and in such a way that its
chances will be as strong as possible.*

Pitt agreed to Wilberforce's request to introduce the
bill, but in hindsight this may not have been a helpful first
step for the cause. The wording of Pitt's motion was not as
strong as it might have been, and his introductory speech
not as forceful as it should have been. Pitt was attempting
to avoid offending the opponents of abolition and did not
make the kind of passionate speech of which Wilberforce
was capable. The fact that the Privy Council committee
had not concluded its hearings meant that most members
felt they lacked sufficient information to take the matter
seriously.

Meanwhile another member of Parliament, Sir William
Dolben, introduced a slave trade bill without coordinating

his efforts with Wilberforce and the main abolition leaders. Dolben's bill would have placed a modest limit on the number of slaves that could be carried on a ship, and this limit would expire in a year. This effort fell far short of ending the slave trade and therefore might not enlist the backing of the strongest abolition voices. Passing the bill would accomplish little, and its defeat could have dire consequences for the earlier bill introduced by Pitt. Had Wilberforce been on the scene, he most likely would have urged Dolben to withhold his measure until the Pitt bill was considered. The Dolben bill passed, but it was tactically harmful to the abolition cause. It allowed members who were not sure about supporting Pitt's bill to be content with their support of the much weaker Dolben bill. It also allowed the first round of parliamentary debate to proceed without the oratorical and tactical strength only Wilberforce could have provided.

Wilberforce was well enough to return to London in November, but a national political crisis delayed further progress on the abolition cause. King George III became physically and mentally ill, and the prospects for his recovery were not good. William Pitt and the Parliament spent months trying to determine if a regent should be appointed to exercise the king's powers until he either recovered or died. The king did recover, but nothing was accomplished on the slave trade issue or much of anything else until well into the new year.

James Stephen was a bright attorney practicing in St. Kitts. He had seen the suffering of slaves in St. Kitts and had considerable knowledge of maritime issues. Wilberforce hoped to attract him to the cause.

Stephen was particularly concerned that the testimony of the slave trade supporters not go unchallenged. So much of it was ridiculous enough that most would not give it serious thought, but some of it was plausible enough to need a serious rebuttal. Stephen's problem was that any open support of Wilberforce's work would be the end of his law practice in St. Kitts, and he had a large family to support. For now, he could only serve as a source of reliable information and tactical advice. He was also willing to help Wilberforce prepare for the debates in the Commons. "Mr. Wilberforce, you are absolutely right in what you are doing. Don't give up, no matter what kind of opposition you may face in the days ahead."

James Stephen's encouragement and help were important in the days to come.

The release of the Privy Council report on the hearings helped provide information to the members, but there were many who wanted members to pay more attention to the testimony of slavery's defenders. Wilberforce worked with Pitt to develop a set of resolutions built on the testimony and continued to work hard to prepare himself for his first presentation of the issue in the Parliament on May 12, 1789.

Speeches on major new issues in the Parliament were often lengthy, and Wilberforce's speech went for more than three hours. He had earned his reputation in politics partly on the basis of his speaking skill, and he was in good form in bringing the issue to the Commons. He intentionally put more emphasis on reason than on speaking style. He traced the slave trade through its course, showing its negative impact on Africa, the loss of life and suffering on the trip across the ocean, and the capacity of the West Indies to continue their plantation economy without new slaves being imported. He drew on the testimony before the Privy Council, using part of it as evidence and rebutting the testimony of supporters of the trade. He had prepared for the speech for weeks, but he spoke from only a few notes. Edmund Burke compared his clarity and force with the legendary orator Demosthenes.

If careful preparation and excellent speaking guaranteed success, the fight against the slave trade would have been a short one, but the debate on the issue continued for days until the defenders of the slave trade succeeded in arguing that the House must constitute itself a committee of the whole to take further evidence and testimony. This tactic was successful in blocking action for the moment. As the session ended, Wilberforce pled with his colleagues to act. "We can no longer plead ignorance," he said, "we cannot turn aside." But that is exactly what the Commons did when it adjourned in late June. There was to be no quick solution to the slave trade question.

nine

People rightfully remember Wilberforce's work on abolition, but from the very beginning of his work on the slave trade, he felt equally called to do something to bring about the reform of many other evils in society, not just to deal with the slavery problem. An October 25, 1787, entry in his journal emphasizes the broad calling that he felt God was giving him at that time. He wrote, "God Almighty has set before me two great objects: the suppression of the slave trade and the reformation of manners."[1]

People gave Wilberforce considerable credit for his work on abolition but forgot that he saw moral reform and abolition as two distinct callings. At the time, he thought both causes could be taken on at the same time and both could succeed in relatively short order. Forty years later, slavery was still legal. His long slavery battle is the one for which he received the greatest blessings or curses. The work on moral reform was actually somewhat successful rather quickly, but the battle against slavery took place in the public's view, and his efforts for moral reformation occurred in less obvious ways.

Those who didn't realize how profound Wilberforce's change of values had been in the course of about two years might have been surprised when they first heard about his work on moral reform. He seemed to be questioning the entire way of life of the wealthy, a way of life he had experienced for years. But that's exactly the point. He had experienced this way of life from childhood through early adulthood until his commitment to Christ. He was now ready to call his countrymen to a higher moral standard.

For the wealthy in the eighteenth century, there were few moral constraints. Gluttony and drunkenness were part of the life of conspicuous consumption. Heavy gambling was another measure of one's wealth. The only constraint on gambling was the expectation that a person pay off his or her losses in due time. The nobleman could be sarcastic and rude to his peers, especially to the lower classes, but must be ready to defend his own honor when insulted, usually by fighting a duel. The noblewoman must produce a male heir, but the husband and wife were both free to be unfaithful to each other, as long as children were produced and properly raised by their domestic staff. The activities of the privileged were those that Wilberforce pursued in his early years—witty conversation, patronage of the arts, generosity in entertaining one's peers, and participation in an endless succession of pleasurable activities.

The poor, of course, were excluded from most of the vices of the wealthy, except for the many glimpses they were given when working as domestic servants. Child labor was common in the early stages of industrialization, causing some to question the efforts to eliminate slavery when working conditions for the poor were so horrible. The poor could not afford the kind of liquor favored by the rich but had plenty of human misery that they might forget while drunk. They couldn't afford to gamble or dine and drink at the expensive clubs, but they had their corresponding diversions, including bullbaiting, cockfighting, and the public execution of criminals. The poor probably were no better or worse than the wealthy in their sexual conduct, in terms of biblical standards.[2]

Abolition had a clear solution: the passage of legislation to outlaw first the slave trade, then slavery itself. No amount of effort toward reform would have been effective as long as slavery was legal. It was different with the moral conditions that agitated Wilberforce at the time. Legislation was not the answer. The evangelical revival movement was certainly aimed toward a complete change of life, away from the vices of the wealthy and the poor; but most of the privileged classes remained untouched by the messages and calls to repentance of evangelical preachers like John Wesley and George Whitefield.

In the campaign for moral reform, Wilberforce decided to fade into the background. He would work quietly gathering political support but leave others in charge of the actual campaign. The first step toward national moral reform, the reissuing of a previous royal proclamation on morals, happened quickly and easily. Wilberforce enlisted the help of his friend and political ally William Pitt, the prime minister. Pitt in turn persuaded the archbishop of Canterbury, John Moore, to carry the request to the royal family. With the support of Queen Charlotte, the archbishop talked with King George III, who readily agreed to reissue the proclamation and did so on June 1, 1787. Because Wilberforce wanted to first enlist the support of national leaders, he insisted that the issuing of the proclamation be done without public notice.

The proclamation's stated purpose was "the encouragement of piety and virtue; and for the preventing of vice, profaneness, and immorality." Much of the text was carried over from previous sovereigns and from George's first proclamation. Some of its statements were very general, calling on the king's subjects to help reform "persons of dissolute and debauched lives." Other statements were very specific, such as the prohibition of gambling on Sunday and mandatory attendance at church. The evils Wilberforce despised were all forbidden in the proclamation—prostitution, excessive gambling, drunkenness, and pornography.

King George added a preamble to the proclamation calling particular attention to the problems of the day:

Whereas we cannot but observe with inexpressible concern, the rapid progress of impiety and licentiousness, and that deluge of profaneness, immorality, and every kind of vice, which to the scandal of our holy religion, and to the evil example of our loving subjects, have broken in upon this nation: We, therefore, have thought fit, by the advice of our Privy Council, to issue this our Royal Proclamation, and do hereby declare our Royal

82

> *purpose and resolution to discountenance and pun-*
> *ish all manner of vice, profaneness, and immorality,*
> *in all persons, of whatsoever degree or quality,*
> *within this our Realm, and particularly in such as*
> *are employed near our Royal Persons. . . .*[3]

If words alone could produce reform, Wilberforce could have taken great comfort in a completed project. He knew that the statement by itself would mean little, though. The text itself contained some means of enforcement. It directed ministers to read the statement at least four times a year after worship. It also directed the sheriffs in each county to enforce the proclamation. But of much greater importance was Wilberforce's continued work behind the scenes to carry out a "top down, bottom up" plan.

The leaders Wilberforce recruited to join the Proclamation Society provided the support he sought at the top level of society. Wilberforce recruited two kinds of persons for this loosely structured association. The first were people of high social standing who were not known as spiritual leaders and not even as great moral role models. Wilberforce asked the duke of Montagu, the Master of the Horse, to be president of the Proclamation Society; the duke's brother, the earl of Ailesbury, to be another member; and the duke of Manchester to join, as well. Wilberforce was conscious that many of his peers thought he had gone overboard with his new evangelical experience and wanted the moral reform movement to have broad support. But other key leaders of the group were Wilberforce's evangelical allies from the abolition movement, Sir Charles Middleton, Edward Eliot, Hannah More, and Henry Thornton.

Wilberforce expanded the "top down" part of the movement to the grass roots level by going from one national leader to another, asking for their support and calling on them to encourage the formation of local efforts to promote the proclamation. From the small core group, the list of Proclamation Society members grew to include numerous bishops and archbishops (most of them more significant for their social than for their spiritual leadership) and a large group of nobles. The "trickle-down" approach actually worked reasonably well. Local constables, parish officers, and church wardens began calling meetings to discuss ways of using the proclamation to generate moral reform.

Previously, the burden for prosecuting criminals fell on the victims, but the momentum shifted toward prosecution for "victimless" crimes, including the examples mentioned in the proclamation—drunkenness, prostitution, and gambling. People came to accept Wilberforce's reasoning that violent crimes, which resulted in endless numbers of public hangings, had their seed in the proliferation of lesser crimes in each community.

Supplementing these organizational efforts, some excellent writers began to call on both the top and bottom levels of society to reform their lives. Hannah More, one of the first members of the Proclamation Society, was a talented playwright and poet and a member of the Blue Stocking literary group in London. She had experienced a conversion experience similar to Wilberforce's and began writing material on spiritual and moral issues. An example of her books calling for the reform of the upper classes was *An Enquiry into the Duties of Men in the Upper and Middle Classes of Society.* She called on members of her own class to become examples of moral living. She also began writing inexpensive tracts directed to the lower classes. She entitled one of her series of tracts *Village Politics,* featuring a character named "Will Chip." Millions of copies of the tracts were sold and read.[4]

Was Wilberforce's work on moral reform successful? There were some indications of improvement in the national morality. A number of highly placed people resigned their memberships in the clubs, becoming regular with family prayers and appropriate observance of the Lord's Day. People began taking their faith more seriously, and the quality of the clergy increased. The number of clergy who simply held their positions for the income, with no thought of providing spiritual leadership, declined. Previously, one would have had to look far and wide in the Church of England to find spiritual strength among its ministers.

Wilberforce left the reform effort's success for God to judge. He saw much evidence of great improvement in the country, for which he took no credit. His goal had been to work quietly but persistently on these tasks, with no one receiving credit or blaming him for what had been done. "My little part for spiritual renewal in England has been quiet, but it may be the greatest legacy of my life," he concluded.

ten

William Wilberforce was a courageous individual who deserves all the credit given him for his efforts on moral reform and slavery, but it would be a serious mistake to describe his work without reference to the individuals who functioned as a very important supportive community to Wilberforce. His spiritual strength depended very much on the encouragement and counsel he received from a number of his contemporaries, and he would have been lost without the many things he received from a Christian residential community, the Clapham community.

The mentoring and encouragement Wilberforce received were a continuation of the help he was given during the initial months of struggle when he was finding himself spiritually. John Newton, who helped Wilberforce understand that he could serve Christ by continuing his career in politics, continued as an encourager for many years. Newton testified during the Privy Council hearings, drawing on his direct knowledge of the slave trade. Newton and Wilberforce saw each other regularly, and there were times when Newton listened sympathetically to Wilberforce's expressions of discouragement and urged him to persist in the work. One of the ways Newton helped Wilberforce was by introducing him to a number of significant persons who became spiritual mentors to Wilberforce, including John Thornton and Hannah More.

One of Wilberforce's spiritual heroes and role models from an earlier generation was John Wesley, whose ministry and work had done so much to call the people of England back to a meaningful personal faith in Christ. Just before Wesley died, he wrote to Wilberforce, urging that he not give up his efforts to bring an end to the "execrable villainy [slavery], which is the scandal of religion, of England, and of human nature." He went on, in what must have been one of the most treasured messages Wilberforce ever received:

> *Unless God has raised you up for this very thing, you will be worn out by the opposition of men and devils, but if God be for you who can be against you? Are all of them together stronger than God? Oh be not weary of well-doing. Go on in the name of God, and in the power of His might, till even American slavery, the vilest that ever saw the sun, shall vanish away before it. That He that has guided you from your youth up may continue to strengthen in this and all things, is the prayer of,*

Dear Sir, Your affectionate servant, John Wesley.[1]

To another of Wilberforce's close friends and spiritual mentors, Hannah More, belongs some credit for helping him find a balance between spiritual intensity and human warmth. Having for years lived a life of "gaiety" as it was called at the time, after committing his life to Christ, Wilberforce was at first inclined to overreact and become overly serious. Hannah More became equally strong in her faith, but she understood the validity of maintaining her friendships and social involvements. "I declare, I think you are serving God by making yourself agreeable. . .to worldly but well-disposed people, who would never be attracted to religion by grave and severe divines," said More to Wilberforce. She helped him understand that he could be a joyful person without compromising his Christian convictions. Hannah never married and continued for many years as a spiritual sister to Wilberforce.[2]

These and other individuals had much to do with Wilberforce's spiritual staying power and his diligence in accomplishing his life goals. But a cluster of Christian leaders at a place called Clapham came to be even more crucial in what he became and what he accomplished. The Clapham group had its roots in a group of evangelicals in Parliament who were sometimes called the "Saints," not always meant as a compliment. Among those evangelicals were Edward Eliot and Henry Thornton.

Henry Thornton had a proposal for Wilberforce. "William, you know that my estate of Battersea Rise is much larger than my family and I need. I'd like you to move here, and I'd like us to think about others who could join us so we could pray together, enjoy fellowship with one another, and work together on important projects for the advancement of the kingdom of God. You know the pressures of public life. This can be a retreat and a place to plan our spiritual battles."

"I agree that the location would be good for me, Thornton, especially while the Parliament is in session. I want to be a bit away from the chaos of Westminster, but not so far as to require long periods of travel. Tell me more of what you have in mind."

Thornton discussed the type of people who might come to live and visit the estate. His brothers Samuel and Robert were there, as were William Smith and Granville Sharp, all people with whom they had worked closely on the abolition effort. By living in close proximity, he hoped they could increase their chances of moving ahead on the slave trade effort. He planned to invite Charles Grant and Edward Eliot to come to Clapham, too.

Battersea Rise was bound to become something of a political strategy center, considering the number of residents who were directly involved in the government, but Thornton's dream was that it become a place where the residents could encourage one another spiritually and be helpful to one another when feeling discouraged.

William Wilberforce accepted Henry Thornton's invitation to move to Clapham and live at Battersea Rise. He lived in the main house for five years, then moved to Broomfield Lodge on the estate when he was married five years later. Wilberforce and the group at Clapham attracted others who were interested in the causes of abolition, moral reform, and numerous other projects such as the

Sierra Leone colony. Later the community came to be called the "Clapham Sect," but this was not an accurate label. This was in no sense a sect, with distinctive or unorthodox beliefs and practices. These were evangelicals who for the most part remained in the Church of England, determined to be a positive spiritual force in the church. They were drawn together by the opportunity for spiritual nourishment, fellowship, intellectual exchange, and political strategizing.

The Clapham community was anything but a place of serenity. Its residents and visitors felt free to seek each other out on issues of mutual interest, which meant they engaged in conversations that went on for hours. The inner circle of the community regularly consulted one another on matters that affected the community itself and their individual lives. Wilberforce called these discussions "Cabinet Councils," giving them a more official sound than was intended. Thornton began adding to Battersea Rise to accommodate the growing numbers of residents and visitors, until it eventually had more than thirty bedrooms. The library designed by Pitt became the focal point of many gatherings of Clapham people.

Henry Thornton was successful in attracting John Venn as the rector for Clapham parish, and Venn became an important part of the attraction of living there. Wilberforce described Venn's ministry: "I like him very much, and if I am not greatly mistaken, you will grow inordinately fond of him." Venn felt the same high regard for Wilberforce, describing him as "no common Christian: His knowledge of divine things and his experience of the power of the gospel are very extraordinary."[3]

Clapham became a concentration of energy that was deployed toward many causes. Wilberforce is best remembered for his work on slavery and moral reform, but he was active in many causes that came from the collective work of people at Clapham. There were numerous humanitarian efforts on behalf of suffering people, including victims of the Napoleonic wars, victims of war in Greece, North American Indians, Haitians, and others. Major outreach efforts of the Church of England were birthed at Clapham, including the Church Missionary Society and the British and Foreign Bible Society. Clapham people gave considerable energy to sustain the Sierra Leone colony and worked hard to improve conditions in the British colony of India. One of the things that made these many efforts possible was the willingness of Claphamites to give of their own resources to these causes. Henry Thornton is said to have contributed five-sixths of his considerable income to these and other causes, and Wilberforce was also extremely generous in his charitable giving.

The intellectual and spiritual interaction among those at Clapham might suggest that it was a somber, joyless place. This was certainly not the case for William Wilberforce. He had taken Hannah More's advice and restored a spirit of joy and exuberance into his life after a period of spiritual introspection and struggle. Before he was married and had children, Wilberforce loved to play with the children of the Clapham community. Henry Thornton's oldest child, Marianne, recalled William's playfulness:

He was as restless and volatile as a child himself, and during the long and grave discussions

that went on between him and my father and oth-
ers he was most thankful to refresh himself by
throwing a ball or a bunch of flowers at me, or
opening the glass door and going off with one for
a race on the lawn "to warm his feet."[4]

Being a part of the Clapham community benefitted William Wilberforce in a number of ways. Before he had his own family, the community was his family. It was a source of help with his major life projects. It provided camaraderie and friendship that took the place of the kind of socializing in the elite clubs that no longer appealed to him. When so little success was experienced in the abolition effort for so many years, Wilberforce could count on receiving encouragement and new ideas from community members. When his health was marginal, there were people nearby to give advice and offer prayer on his behalf. In short, Clapham was the single most important factor in Wilberforce's intellectual contentment, his political accomplishments, and his spiritual nourishment. It was vital to him, and he was important in attracting other outstanding leaders to live there or visit.

eleven

I f Wilberforce had only been able to relate successfully with fellow Christians, the impact of his lifework would undoubtedly have been limited. Surrounded as he was by a group of amiable and gifted persons at the Clapham community, he might have chosen to give his entire attention to these like-minded persons. His inner circle of people, those whom he trusted the most and felt closest to, were the fellow believers he knew in politics and in other careers, but Wilberforce never isolated himself within the circle of Christians he knew. He interacted with nonbelievers throughout his life, and these relationships were essential to his accomplishments.

Former U.S. Senator (R-Oregon) Mark Hatfield wrote the introduction to one of the editions of Wilberforce's book *Real Christianity*. In the introduction, Senator Hatfield said it was striking to discover Wilberforce's book and see that he had, without realizing it, modeled his own life and career after the great British politician. The two statesmen, one British and one American, had much in common, including a conversion experience after they had entered a political career. One of the things that struck Hatfield about Wilberforce was that he put great stock in dealing with others in a respectful and caring way, whether or not these persons shared his Christian values. Wilberforce "sought to continue the incarnation of the Word in loving acts of mercy, justice, and charity to those around him, even if they were adversaries."[1]

Those who knew Hatfield would say the same about his interaction with colleagues during a long political career. They both had their closest relationships with fellow believers, but both followed the example of Christ in relating lovingly to nonbelievers. If someone had a personal need, they responded in a caring, prayerful manner. If it was a spiritual need, they sought to offer counsel and prayer. If it was a physical need, they responded with empathy. In short, they rejected the self-centeredness and arrogance that is so typically found among politicians.

Wilberforce often visited his friend Hannah More at Bath. Others went there for the marvelous waters, but what brought him back was the chance to drink together of the water of Life, so to speak. He remembered her advice about not becoming too intense and sober, risking turning people away from the kingdom of God, not drawing them into it. Because of her advice, he found a way to bring a measure of joyful exuberance alongside the self-discipline of the Christian life.

They discussed the difficulty of creating an opportunity to talk with people about what it means to be a believer. "We talk about politics, about social events, we gossip about the foibles of the royal family and the rich, we talk about the weather, about the theater, but why do people not want to think about things of eternal importance?" Wilberforce wondered.

"I suppose we have to earn the right to be heard as a result of the spiritual qualities we demonstrate," Hannah replied. "We have to care about those around us, so they will see the love of Christ through our interest. How have you been trying to turn your conversations toward spiritual things?"

Wilberforce realized that the Holy Spirit might lead him to someone he didn't even know who was spiritually hungry. He prayed each day that he would be ready to speak to people seeking the Lord. He also kept a list of people he knew who were not believers and prayed over that list regularly, asking the Holy Spirit to open their hearts to consider their spiritual needs. "I certainly haven't given up on our friend Pitt, but I suppose there are others on the list more open to thinking about God than he seems to be."

Wilberforce had decided he couldn't just wait for openings—he needed to make them. He had been experimenting with what he called "launchers," questions or comments that might steer the conversation away from trivial things to matters of eternal consequence. In a few cases, his launching comment was something like, "You and I spent considerable time together in times past, didn't we?" The response might be something like, "Yes, we did, but we're older now, and things have changed." Then he would say something like, "You're so right that things have changed, and for my part I don't regret a bit that things have changed." This gave him a chance to talk about the great change in his life that came from being a devoted follower of Christ. That didn't guarantee they wanted to hear about it, but at least the subject was opened.

The desire of both Hannah More and William Wilberforce to let others know what it meant to be a follower of Christ sometimes bore fruit. They and their Clapham friends had an impact on the elite in British society that went well beyond the response to the evangelical preachers of the day. But inevitably, many who respected Wilberforce for his new spiritual convictions showed no desire to adopt the same way of life. William Pitt was one of the first to hear Wilberforce's testimony as a believer, but he closed the door on the invitation to follow him into the life of faith. Pitt remained adamant in his resistance to being evangelized. Nevertheless, the mutual respect and friendship that had drawn the two of them together early in their careers continued until Pitt's death in 1806. William Wilberforce deserves much of the credit for the durability of their relationship, for they experienced a series of stressful interactions that easily could have alienated them.

Topping the list of political disagreements between William Pitt and William Wilberforce was their disagreement over the continuance of the war with France in the 1790s, one of the outgrowths of the French Revolution. The issue was not whether war was an appropriate response to a challenge from one's enemies. Wilberforce was not a pacifist, but he saw much to be lost from continuing this particular war.

He accurately predicted that the war would preoccupy the British government for years to come, making it virtually impossible to deal with the slave trade and parliamentary reform. The radicalism that characterized French politics made it easy for the conservatives in England to warn against changing the political status quo. Wilberforce also feared that his efforts toward the moral reform of British society would be undercut by the war with France, but actually the brutal fate of the French aristocracy provided a warning to their counterparts in England that resisting moral reform was the wrong direction to take.[2]

Wilberforce felt sure that Pitt would be upset if his friend publicly opposed his stand on the war, but Wilberforce offered an amendment in the House that called on the government to seek peace. Pitt opposed the amendment, and it was soundly defeated. Wilberforce lost sleep over the action he had taken, still believing it had been right but finding it hard to deal with the prime minister's anger. Pitt in turn lost sleep over the breach in the relationship and puzzled over whether Wilberforce, whose courage and good judgment he admired, had been right on this one. After some weeks during which the political and personal rift between the two was painfully apparent to those around them, they cooperated with friends who got them back together socially. They determined to continue working together, in spite of the likelihood that Wilberforce might again be forced to put conviction ahead of friendship.[3]

A second clash between the two men was of shorter duration, and Wilberforce demonstrated that he possessed some of the same pragmatism and flexibility that typified Pitt's approach to politics. The notion of defending one's honor when opponents crossed an imaginary line between debate and insult was widely accepted in English culture at the time. In this case, Pitt accused a fellow member of Parliament, George Tierney, of intentionally undermining British foreign policy. The Speaker of the House ruled the comments inappropriate, but Pitt refused to back down. The verbal battle quickly escalated from a confrontation into the threat of a duel. Neither of the men was willing to back off, and the duel actually occurred. Fortunately for both, neither was a good marksman, and perhaps neither actually intended to kill the other. By the unwritten rules of dueling, the exchange of two shots with no casualties was sufficient to end the duel and restore the honor of both men, so they were able to return to the city with the matter settled formally, if not relationally.

Wilberforce reacted swiftly to the news of the duel. He was already annoyed at Pitt for his lack of cooperation on the slave trade issue. Wilberforce was appalled at the barbarism of dueling and incensed that they would corrupt the Sabbath with such activity. Prudence would have suggested that Wilberforce talk privately with Pitt about the matter before taking action, but Wilberforce did not do this. Instead, he talked with people in London about the issue and found support for a measure to outlaw dueling. He quickly gave notice of his intent to introduce the bill. By evening Pitt had written a letter to Wilberforce that was cordial on the surface but explosive in its tone and content. Pitt asserted that pursuing the antidueling motion was the same as moving for Pitt's removal as prime minister, since Pitt had been one of the duelers who had prompted the measure.

Wilberforce dropped his bill by the end of the week, conceding that he had no desire to bring down the Pitt government, with which he agreed most of the time. He assured Pitt that he didn't want to cause that kind of political damage. In doing so, Wilberforce couldn't resist including a statement in his letter addressing Pitt's spiritual need: "It is my sincere prayer, my dear Pitt, that you may here be the honored instrument of Providence for your country's good, and for the well-being of the civilized world; and much more that you may at length partake of a more solid and durable happiness and honor than this world can bestow."[4]

A third and final political clash between the two men occurred not long before Pitt's death. Lord Melville, Henry Dundas, long a close political ally of Pitt, had been appointed head of the British navy. In 1805 a Committee of Navy Inquiry presented a report charging Melville with the knowledge of or responsibility for the misuse of public funds when Melville had been treasurer of the Navy. Opposition members of Parliament seized on the report to discredit the Pitt government, and the two sides engaged in a long verbal battle in Parliament. Wilberforce listened carefully to the debate, seeking some justification for remaining silent and not adding fuel to the anti-Pitt vehemence. Feeling he may have been impulsive in the dueling case, Wilberforce thought long and hard about what to do in this new situation involving Pitt. Such debates often carried on long into the night, and this was no exception. At 4:00 A.M., Wilberforce rose to speak. As he did, he saw the look in Pitt's eyes, a look pleading that he not lend his eloquence to the side about to impeach Melville. Wilberforce's talk was short and to the point, expressing contempt for Melville's unethical conduct. Prior to his speech, the expectation was that the government's position would prevail. After the speech, the vote was a tie. The Speaker cast the deciding vote to impeach Melville.

Pitt was devastated by the defeat and hurt by Wilberforce's role in the outcome. Some were ready to blame Wilberforce for Pitt's subsequent physical and emotional collapse, which led to his death at an early age. But the evidence does not support this speculation. Their friendship survived the disagreement, and they were reconciled. Because they had, for the most part, interacted fairly and respectfully in spite of their very different political approaches and spiritual values, the way remained open for them to be friends and colleagues.

twelve

G entlemen, you've had a chance to read my report about my patient, William Wilberforce," said Dr. Richard Warren, one of the most prominent physicians of his day. "He hasn't even reached age thirty, but I'll be honest with you, with this many things wrong with him, I'm not optimistic that he will live another year."

"I think his chances are considerably worse than you say," offered a colleague. "Barring some major change in his body or some dramatic results from treatment, I wouldn't give him more than two weeks."

Wilberforce was not blessed with a strong physical heredity. Only one of his three sisters survived into adulthood. William was small of stature, had poor eyesight, and—considering his youthful overindulgence in food and drink—it was remarkable that his health problems were not more severe. His eye problems probably hindered his success during his university days, but his lack of serious motivation was a greater barrier to success than his eyesight. When Wilberforce turned from a life of indulgence to a much more self-disciplined lifestyle, he probably took some additional health risks. A doctor who examined him after his conversion experience warned him that fasting for spiritual purposes could have serious physical consequences for a person who was not physically strong. Then when Wilberforce sought to make up for his earlier study habits by spending hours reading, his doctor warned that his already poor eyesight could deteriorate even further. The doctor's prescription was one of the most common in that day: that Wilberforce go to Bath to partake of the mineral water there.[1]

The waters of Bath were of some help, but Wilberforce's health continued to deteriorate in early 1788. He became ill in early January, but he was at a crucial point in preparing for the Privy Council hearings on the slave trade and refused to slow down. He tried to keep going with his responsibilities during February and March, but his symptoms of high fever, terrible intestinal pain, insomnia, and weakness continued. Sometimes he went to bed to get some rest, but he was unwilling to follow the advice of his family and friends to get away from the stresses of his work in London. Instead, he took the advice of his doctors and began taking opium for his pain.

No single aspect of William Wilberforce's life is as puzzling to us as his use of opium. He improved rapidly when he began taking the drug in 1788 and continued its use the rest of his life. We might be inclined to think of him as an addict, but it's important to interpret his medicinal use of opium in the context of his times. A variety of medications that contained opium, as well as pure opium itself, were readily available without prescription and were commonly used. Opium was an ingredient of a syrup given to babies and a tonic used by children. No one at the time felt that Wilberforce, an evangelical Christian, was compromising his Christian witness by using the drug.

Wilberforce did hesitate before going ahead with the use of opium, not on moral or spiritual grounds, but because its effects were not well understood and it was clear that he could never stop taking the drug. Medical professionals today would describe Wilberforce's ailment as ulcerative colitis. In the context of what was known about the illness and the available treatments, his doctors' recommendation was probably appropriate. The principal hazard would have been taking the opium for its narcotic effect and gradually increasing the dosage. This would have been easy to do, since it was readily available. But Wilberforce did not begin taking the drug for psychological reasons. He needed relief from the pain, and his doctors advised him on the amounts he should take. Even though he had health problems for the rest of his life and continued taking opium for forty-five years, he was able to keep the dosage at an appropriate level, only increasing it temporarily when he had unusual symptoms. There was no question that he was dependent on the drug, just as diabetics must have insulin to stay alive, but Wilberforce was not an addict in any modern sense.

The issue of harmful side effects from taking opium would have been impossible for Wilberforce to consider, since almost nothing was known about it at the time. Today a physician would be concerned about negative effects on his already poor eyesight. Indeed, his eyes became progressively worse. Some of this could have been from his long hours of intense study and the limited knowledge of corrective lenses and corrective surgery. But he also probably hurt his eyes because of his regular opium use. He became more absentminded in later years and had more trouble being diligent about his duties. But looking at his life accomplishments, his long service in the Parliament, and his being able to live into his seventies, one could hardly make a case for serious physical and emotional deterioration from the drug.

Even though Wilberforce improved considerably in March 1788, and the work on the slave trade hearings in the Parliament was at a crucial stage, he realized how close he had come to dying. Rather than risk another relapse from the stress of continuing his work in London, he decided to take the advice of his family and doctors to get away to Bath. His willingness to disengage himself at the time and to call on Prime Minister Pitt to offer the first slave trade motion was a measure of his good sense and his confidence that others in the abolition movement would carry on the work until he could return.

Probably more important for Wilberforce's recovery than the waters of Bath and the use of opium was his willingness to set aside his worries about the abolition struggle and spend time in complete rest and solitude. He wrote about the healing effects of reading the Bible and praying "early in the fine autumn mornings when the lake used to be as calm as so much glass, and all the mountains, shrouded with vapors, compassed me round like so many sleeping lions. . . ." He wrote a prayer in his journal as he was emerging from the physical and emotional pain that had almost ruined him: "O Lord our God, Thou has said unto us I will never leave you, nor forsake you. . .Thou has supported my spirit in the days of trouble, and has given me many intervals of refreshment, renewing Thy loving kindness day by day. . . ."[2]

thirteen

Wilberforce had been thinking of going to France to see if anyone in that country might be willing to push for the simultaneous abolition of the slave trade. As long as France was standing by to take over the English place in the trade, it would be difficult to get Parliament and the king to pass the slave trade measure. Not only would England lose the slave trade revenue, it would lose it to an old enemy.

Wilberforce's friend Clarkson thought Wilberforce was being horribly naive to think he could go over and make private inquiries. He was a member of Parliament, and his name was well known. The government would soon become aware of his mission and be offended by his self-proclaimed diplomacy. The French revolutionary forces would welcome him with open arms, and that in itself would make him an enemy in the king's palace.

"You may be right, Clarkson," Wilberforce admitted, "but you're the only other one who can undertake this mission. This is absolutely crucial to our cause, no matter what happens to the French government. You've got to go and you've got to find those who might begin to lay the groundwork for doing in France what we hope to do in England. We've got to win the day in our own government, but we can't let our opponents win the game by always playing the French card."

Clarkson was at first encouraged by the support for abolition he found among French liberals. He sent Wilberforce reports about the numerous leaders who agreed that the ideals fueling the French Revolution were directly applicable to the evils of slavery. But he soon encountered the same distrust of the British that mirrored the English dislike of the French. People in France asked Clarkson if he could assure them that the English would pass the abolition measure if the French did. Even though he believed that Parliament would ultimately pass the abolition measure, there was no way he could guarantee when it might pass and certainly no way to predict that French action would become a key factor in the English taking similar action.

When Parliament reconvened in January 1790, Wilberforce once again had to deal with the tactics of his opponents, who wanted to prolong the process by asking for more hearings. The proslavery witnesses expected to go first in the hearings and hoped to exhaust the patience of House members before the proponents got a fair hearing. Wilberforce proposed an alternative process, referring the matter to a special committee. Knowing antiabolition forces would argue that referring the matter to a small committee would limit their right to be heard, Wilberforce proposed that the committee open its sessions to all members who wanted to listen and speak. Some members might take this opportunity at first, but they would eventually lose interest. Then the committee could proceed with gathering evidence.

Wilberforce's procedural tactics were successful. He outmaneuvered those who wanted to block any further consideration of the issue and got the House to refer it to a select committee. He and fellow member William Smith chaired the hearings that continued for many months and gathered thousands of pages of material. Antiabolition witnesses had heard most of the abolition arguments and built a case they considered to be strong. They argued that the slaves were mostly criminals and prisoners of war, deserving very little sympathy. They asserted that there were no commercial opportunities in Africa, apart from the slave trade. And they insisted that life on the slave ships was not as miserable as abolitionists had claimed.

Opponents of abolition did their best to wear down the committee and minimize the chances for the abolitionists to respond, continuing their testimony into April. Wilberforce had his trusted ally Thomas Clarkson at his side in the hearings, preparing responses to the points being made and sometimes going to check on facts and locate additional witnesses. When proslavery testimony ended in April, antiabolitionists tried to get the House to act on the measure immediately. Wilberforce won a second tactical victory, blocking the motion to take up the abolition measure before further testimony.

Even though Parliament adjourned before all the abolitionist testimony could be presented, abolitionists felt they

111

had effectively responded to the proslave-trade forces. Moreover, the hearings generated interest in the question and the public began to take note of the morality of slavery through popularly available material. Numerous pamphlets called on the people to understand the evils of the slave trade. Abolitionists circulated many copies of a detailed sketch Thomas Clarkson had prepared, showing the unbelievable crowding on the slave ships. Many people read and were moved by William Cowper's poem "The Negro's Complaint" which contained the lines, "Is there, as ye sometimes tell us, Is there one who reigns on high? Has He bid you buy and sell us speaking from His throne, the sky?" Abolitionists circulated an edition of the poem, calling on readers to talk about it over tea. In still another medium, Josiah Wedgwood, the great ceramicist of his day, designed a cameo depicting an African slave pleading for mercy. Its inscription was meant to generate compassion and guilt: "Am I Not a Man and a Brother?"[1]

Growing public concern about slavery was Wilberforce's main asset when Prime Minister Pitt called a national election in 1790. Wilberforce had some concerns about how he would fare in the election. He feared that his heavy involvement in the slave trade issue, the difficulty of getting back to Yorkshire as often as he thought he should, and the difficulty he experienced in keeping up with his constituents' correspondence might all work against him. But he participated in the canvass, and at the end of three weeks it was clear that he and his fellow incumbent, Henry Duncombe, had ample support to make a challenge impossible. The election came at a good time for Wilberforce, in a way, assuring him he had the backing of his constituents to proceed with the abolition effort.

"Wilberforce, it's clear from the discussions we have already had how much we have in common. It's also clear that you've got some problems with your eyesight that would make it hard to get through the piles of material presented to the Privy Council and then to the select committee. I think Thomas Gisborne will be happy to make room for us at Yoxall Lodge, where we both would be free of distractions. I can read over the material more quickly than you can. We can discuss it, make notes, and get ready for the next round of hearings and debates. I can set aside other projects for as long as it takes to work on this and for as many hours a day as we can productively deal with it."

"Babington, that's exactly what I need. I need a quiet place, and I need the help of someone like you to think through what may still be lacking in our case. I think you are a wonderful gift from God for the work that needs to be done."

Had Wilberforce and Babington known that the decade of the 1790s would see one defeat after another for the abolition cause in Parliament, it might have been hard to spend so much time in preparing their case. But the formidable challenges ahead called for all the effort and intellectual strength they could muster. The first of these challenges was the news of a slave uprising in Santo Domingo (later called the Dominican Republic). There were ten times as many slaves in the colony as white colonists, and there was a large group of mulattos who took the side of the slaves in the revolt. The revolt was unsuccessful, but two thousand whites were killed, and the incident gave the proslavery faction in Parliament a chance to argue that the abolition effort was directly responsible for slave unrest. A proslavery member of Parliament claimed, without solid evidence, that the slaves acted on the assumption that Wilberforce and his allies would eventually succeed in freeing them. Even though the abolitionists' objective was simply to cut off the transport of slaves, the proslave voices seized on the uprising to argue that peace and economic stability in the West Indies was threatened by the debate on abolition.

Whether or not he thought he could immediately succeed, Wilberforce put all his rhetorical skill and energy into the debate on the floor of the Commons in 1791. The debate began in the late afternoon on April 18 and continued with only short recesses until the early hours of April 20. Like his first major speech on the subject two years before, this was a long one, lasting four hours. He used the months of preparation to good advantage, restating the moral high ground he had earlier claimed and answering the points made in the hearings by the defenders of the slave trade. He spoke of new evidence of cruelty in the seizure of slaves before their transport and new reports of despicable conditions during their shipment. He argued that the West Indian planters had falsely asserted that the colonies could not survive without a steady supply of new slaves. In fact, he said, eliminating the supply would motivate the planters to treat the existing slaves more humanely, and a healthier population of slaves would assure their numbers would continue to be sufficient and diminish the likelihood that they might revolt.

Hours of debate followed Wilberforce's opening speech. Numerous defenders of slavery spoke. Strong voices took the abolition side, including those of William Pitt, Charles James Fox, and Edmund Burke. A few members declared their intention of shifting to the abolition side of the vote. But concerns about developments in France and fears of the slave revolt in Dominica turned the sentiment in the House against the abolition case. There were some sixty members with direct ties to shipping and to the West Indian colonies, and they voted as a block against Wilberforce. The result was a crushing defeat: 163 "no" votes and 88 "yea" votes.

A pragmatist would have taken the defeat as reason enough to suspend the abolition efforts for a more promising time. Wilberforce was not a pragmatist. He made it clear after the 1791 defeat that he would continue pursuing the cause every year, no matter how little progress there was toward succeeding. His determination gave courage to the abolition movement and gave birth to a new kind of local support network, what we would call grassroots lobbying. The Committee for the Abolition of the Slave Trade organized local abolition associations around the country. The national committee provided information to the local groups by preparing and distributing a one-volume summary of the massive amount of material presented at the slave trade hearings. Local enthusiasts began circulating petitions against the slave trade and delivering these to Parliament. This was not common practice in that day, and even Wilberforce wondered whether this kind of popular expression to the Parliament was appropriate. Even more radical in the minds of some was the local abolitionists' organizing of sugar boycotts. As mild as this action might appear to modern observers, it certainly wasn't standard practice at the time, and it raised fears associated with the expressions of radical democracy in France.

Principled reformers sometimes find their greatest challenge among their supporters, those who profess belief in their cause but advocate a cautious and gradual approach to change. This was the fate of the abolition movement in 1792. True to his word after his defeat the year before, Wilberforce presented his abolition measure in April 1792, again accompanied by a powerful speech. He ended it with a statement of gratitude that even though not successful, he "had the bliss of remembering that he had demanded justice for millions who could not ask it for themselves."[2] Judging from the vote the year before, the chances of getting the bill passed were not good. Then Henry Dundas rose to speak, expressing support for the measure but proposing to amend it by inserting one word, the word *gradual* before abolition. He intended that English ships would no longer be allowed to carry slaves to foreign destinations but would be given until 1800 to continue transporting slaves to English-controlled destinations. Later the date was moved to 1796.

One might commend Dundas for practicing the politics of the possible, but for Wilberforce and his strongest supporters, even a delay of four years was unacceptable. At the time they had no way of knowing that abolition would not succeed until a number of years after 1796. They accepted Dundas's profession of belief in the evil of the slave trade but feared a modest delay could lead to a series of postponements. It was the classic struggle of reform movements between idealists and pragmatists, those who wanted change immediately and those who felt a gradual shift was sufficient. Interestingly, William Pitt, who at times was hesitant about continuing to back abolition, attacked Dundas's moderate amendment. He described the amendment as essentially a defeat of abolition. In spite of his efforts, the amendment passed easily, and the amended motion passed 230 to 85, the number of the opponents almost the same as the supporters the previous year. As if doing Wilberforce's work for him, the House of Lords let the measure die.[3]

The war with France that began in 1793 had a devastating effect on the abolition effort because of the old argument that France would step in to operate the slave trade if and when England withdrew from it. Moreover, differing views about the need for war and of its continuance pushed most other business off the agenda in Parliament. So desperate was Wilberforce to keep his issue alive that he actually offered Dundas's gradual measure in 1793, but even that failed to pass either the House of Commons or the House of Lords. One could almost call Wilberforce a fanatic on the slave trade issue, for he tried some form of it every year during the remainder of the 1790s, even though his prospects for success were dim. In 1793 and 1794 he tried a variation on Dundas's bill directing that slaves could not be carried to other nations, but the traffic could continue to English soil. Even with this modest change, he was unsuccessful.

In 1796 and during each of the remaining years of the century, Wilberforce returned to his original effort to completely and immediately abolish the slave trade. The number of members voting was small each of these years, reflecting the lack of interest in the subject, and the margin of defeat varied from year to year, but there was no real sign of hope. One of the most discouraging votes was in 1796, when the vote was scheduled on the evening that a new opera was opening in London. Only 144 members voted, and Wilberforce lost by four votes.

As the century ended, the prospects for abolition were not at all good. Thomas Clarkson, one of the most able workers in the movement outside Parliament, was in poor health and dropped out of the movement. Most of the other members of the Committee to Abolish the Slave Trade had become discouraged, and the committee no longer met regularly. Prime Minister Pitt had fought hard against the Dundas effort to delay abolition, but in 1797, he supported a measure that would have given the assemblies in the West Indian colonies the authority to decide about allowing slaves to be imported. This would have given Pitt a chance to appear supportive of a form of abolition but would do nothing to reduce the trade. No one in the colonial legislatures had any intention of restricting slavery.

The battles had been intense, and the astounding thing was that Wilberforce clung to hope, kept his physical condition stable, and remained in relatively good spirits. Much of the credit for his good spirits can be attributed to the resiliency of his spiritual life, particularly the tactical and spiritual help he received from his colleagues in the Clapham community. Only unshakable hope grounded in his Christian convictions could have kept Wilberforce going during this decade. Only his extraordinarily intense determination could have helped him look ahead to the day when he would succeed.

fourteen

H annah, there is a subject I would like to raise with you," Wilberforce said to his old friend. "You are a gifted writer, and I certainly am not, but almost from the moment I began trying to explain to others my convictions as a serious follower of Christ, I have felt I needed to do more than just talk to people. I think I should begin to put my thoughts on paper in some form. What do you think?"

"That's a fascinating idea, William. Whom would you be addressing with this work?"

"One type of reader would be some of my peers, like William Pitt, who have listened politely to my talk about giving their lives in surrender to Christ as Savior but have never been convinced it is something they should do. I would also hope that my book might affect some people the way Philip Doddridge's book affected me."

"What encouragement have you had from your Christian friends about this project? Have the folks at Clapham had helpful comments on your undertaking?"

"I've talked with Henry Thornton, John Venn, and William Farish. They didn't try to discourage me from going ahead with the work, but I didn't really get much help from them on the content," Wilberforce admitted.

"Could you tell me in a few sentences what you feel God would have you say to your readers? This is to be a book about spiritual things, not about politics, I assume."

"My main message would be that many of those who call themselves Christians fall far short of living out the essence of real Christianity. As long as we allow this inadequate form of Christianity to go unchallenged, those who are spiritually needy will never come to faith in Jesus Christ. Our nation faces many challenges at home and abroad, and now is the time for us to return to a radical faith in Jesus Christ."

"William, just remember that you're a politician, not a theologian. Don't engage in debates with philosophers and scholars. Talk from your heart to those who are spiritually hungry. Your readers must be common people. And don't get tempted to wander into discussing the political issues of the day. Those will come and go. Your spiritual message is a timeless one. Even as passionate as you are about slavery, don't use this book to beat that drum."

It is quite remarkable that Wilberforce was able to follow through on his desire to write something substantial about what it means to be a real Christian. Even though there was somewhat of a lull in the abolition struggle, he continued to work on the cause and introduced numerous bills on the slave trade during the four years he worked on his book. He had the reputation of being a brilliant extemporaneous speaker but lacked the self-discipline to prepare meticulously for major speeches. Constituents and other politicians constantly sought him out with a variety of requests. He received a large amount of correspondence and struggled without success to keep up with it. Although his neighbors at Clapham stimulated his mind and soul and brought him much enjoyment, it was not a place where one could get a significant writing project done. His health was almost always marginal, and his medications had some bad side effects.

Wilberforce was able to write a major book for one reason alone: He was passionate about articulating his faith in Christ. He was as committed to thoroughgoing moral and spiritual reform as he was to ending slavery. He wanted people to understand that Christianity is not about religious respectability. It is first and last the transformation of one's heart and life that makes one live in a loving way. It is living a holy and righteous life and making one's conduct fit the content of their prayers and Bible readings on Sunday.

"What do you have here, Mr. Wilberforce?" publisher Thomas Cadell asked when Wilberforce showed him the manuscript of his book. "Is this about slavery?"

"No, this is not about abolition or any other political issue of the day. Take a look at the title, *A Practical View of the Prevailing Religious System of Professed Christians in the Higher and Middle Classes in this Country Contrasted with Real Christianity.* I think the title pretty well expresses the contents of the piece."

"If you were a religious scholar writing about religion, we would consider it. Since you are a politician of considerable repute, we could publish almost anything you write on national policy issues. But a book on religion by a politician? This is a very long manuscript. My guess is that it would run almost five hundred pages in length. This would be an expensive book to publish. Leave it with me, Wilberforce. I will at least read it and give it some thought. No guarantees, you understand."

"I understand. I'm not asking you to lose money on the book, but give it a careful look. These are hard times in our nation. I think there are many people who are looking for a spiritual anchor in turbulent times."

The first part of Wilberforce's book seems to have a negative tone, for Wilberforce sets about to identify and dismiss widespread views he deemed to be inadequate—views of the character of Christianity itself, of human nature, and of the nature of God. A sample of his criticism of nominal Christians is this statement early in the book:

> With Christianity, professing Christians are little acquainted. Their views of Christianity have been so cursory and superficial that they have little more than perceived those exterior circumstances that distinguish it from other forms of religion. These circumstances are some few facts, and perhaps some leading doctrines and principles, of which they cannot be wholly ignorant. But of the consequences, relations, and practical uses of these

principles, they have few ideas—or none at all.[1]

Amid his attacks on lukewarm Christians there is a warm, positive tone to some of the passages. For example:

If we look to the most eminent of the Scripture characters, we find them warm, zealous, and affectionate. When engaged in their favorite work of celebrating the goodness of their supreme bene-factor, their souls appear to burn within them, and their hearts kindle into rapture. The powers of language are inadequate to express their trans-ports of delight. They call on all nature to swell the chorus, and to unite with them in hallelujahs of gratitude, joy, and praise.[2]

There are also passages that point the way to an imme-diate and compelling relationship with God, such as the following:

Let us have daily intercourse with Him in prayer and praise, seeking dependence and confi-dence in dangers, and hope and joy in our brighter hours. Let us endeavor to keep Him con-stantly in our minds, and to render all our thought of Him more distinct, lively, and intelligent. . . . The name of Jesus is not to be to us like Allah of the Mohammedans; or like a talisman or an amulet, worn on the arm as an external badge and symbol of a profession, thought to preserve one from evil by some mysterious and unintelligible potency. Instead, we should allow the name of Jesus to be engraved deeply on the heart, written there by the finger of God Himself in everlasting characters. It is our sure and undoubted title to present peace and future glory. The assurance which this title conveys of a bright turning toward heaven will lighten the burdens and alleviate the sorrows of life.[3]

Even though Wilberforce told his publisher this was not a book about politics, he ended it with a call to national revival, reform, and prayer:

Boldly I must confess that I believe the national difficulties we face result from the decline of religion and morality among us. I must confess equally boldly that my own solid hopes for the well-being of my country depend, not so much on her navies and armies, nor on the wisdom of her rulers, nor on the spirit of her people, as on the persuasion that she still contains many who love and obey the gospel of Christ. I believe that their prayers may yet prevail. . . . May there be here at least a sanctuary, a land of true faith and piety, where we may still enjoy the blessings of Christianity. May there be here in this nation a place where the name of Christ is still honored and men may see the blessings of faith in Jesus. May the means of religious education and consolation once again be extended to surrounding countries and to the world at large.[4]

In spite of the publisher's pessimism, Wilberforce's book was phenomenally successful. Few today would argue that it has the literary quality and spiritual depth of a book like C. S. Lewis's *Mere Christianity*, but Wilberforce's book took the country by storm. Within the first few days, the first printing was gone, and in a few months 7,500 copies were sold. During Wilberforce's lifetime, the book went through fifteen editions in England and twenty-five in the United States. Translations were published in French, Italian, Spanish, Dutch, and German.

At a time when success in the abolition effort was elusive, the warm praise of friends and strangers alike was a great encouragement to Wilberforce. Sir John Pennington Muncaster wrote to him, "As a friend I thank you for it; as a man I doubly thank you; but as a member of the Christian world, I render you all gratitude and acknowledgment. I thought I knew you well, but I know you better now, my dearest excellent Wilber." John Newton wrote, "I have devoured it. I think you know by this time that I do not much deal in ceremonials and compliments—but I should stifle the feeling of my heart were I wholly to suppress mentioning the satisfaction, the pleasure, the joy, your publication has given me." Edmund Burke's doctor reported his patient spent much of the last two days of his life reading the book and found great comfort in it.[5]

Another prominent figure, Arthur Young, known for his innovative approaches to agriculture, wrote to Wilberforce that he had purchased the book in a time of distress over the suffering and death of his young daughter. He said he read it over and over, and "it made so much impression on me that I scarcely knew how to lay it aside." He said it had drawn him to repentance and into a new relationship with the "great physician of souls."[6]

A somewhat exaggerated report about the book stated, "It was read at the same moment, by all the leading persons in the nation. An electric shock could not be felt more vividly and instantaneously. Everyone talked about it. . . . It was acknowledged that such an important book had not appeared for a century."[7] Even discounting the hyperbole in the statement, Wilberforce had much to be thankful for in having found the time to write the book, in being faithful to the message he felt God had given him, and in expressing it with the same passion that energized his political efforts.

fifteen

Wilberforce's close friend Henry Thornton had recently married, and Wilberforce could clearly see how happy Thornton was in his new life as a husband. Previously Wilberforce had been too busy to even think of marrying. In addition, his health had been so poor that he did not think marriage would be fair to the woman involved, who would end up more of a nurse than a wife. He mentioned his thoughts to his trusted friend Thomas Babington.

"Babington, some weeks ago Henry and I were talking about the idea that it might be good for me to consider marriage. He and Marianne could not be happier. If they can find such wonderful companionship, do you think God has someone for me?"

"What kind of person might win your heart, William?"

"How can I know, if I've never met such a person? But of course I haven't really been looking. First of all, I'm not interested in someone whose only goal is to bring honor to herself and her family by being linked with someone who has some prominence in public life. Likewise, I don't want to consider someone who mainly wants to better herself financially. The one thing I would put above these concerns would be that this person be a good fit spiritually. Nothing would make me happier than to find someone who was as serious as I try to be in following God day by day."

Babington immediately thought of Barbara Spooner, the oldest daughter of Isaac and Barbara Spooner. She was much younger than Wilberforce—about to turn twenty-one—but an interesting and serious young woman.

Exactly two days after Babington and Wilberforce talked about the subject, William received a letter from Barbara Spooner. She said nothing about having heard about him from Thomas Babington, but the timing would suggest that Babington had something to do with her letter. Rather than expressing any interest in meeting him or asking about his political projects, she asked for spiritual advice. This confirmed what Babington had said about her being intent on knowing and following God's will, and it made a deep impression on Wilberforce.

Babington may have also arranged a time for the two to meet each other at a dinner party the very night Wilberforce got the letter. William's entry in his diary after their meeting was appropriately understated, "Pleased with Miss Spooner."[1] During his time at church the next day, on Easter Sunday, he gave up on fully concentrating on worshiping the risen Savior. He confided in his diary at the end of the day that he mingled his adoration of God with his complete infatuation with Barbara Spooner. In literally a day's time he had gone from being intrigued with this person he had not yet met to fantasizing about being married to her.

The expression "whirlwind courtship" hardly does justice to the pace of the romance between William and Barbara during the week after they first met. William was thirty-eight, nearly twice the age of Barbara, but he pursued her like a boy just out of puberty. Thomas Babington served as their escort for their first official date, and from that point the two were together almost every day for the rest of the week. They dined together at the Pump Room and at the Spooners' house. By Saturday, exactly a week after they first met, Wilberforce was saying in his journal that he was totally in love.

"Babington, I want to thank you again for helping me make the acquaintance of Barbara. It's only been a few days since we talked about the idea of my meeting someone I might marry. You were absolutely right that she fits all the things that are important to me in a life companion. This has been an utterly amazing week since we met."

"William, I don't have any reason to think that you aren't right for each other. But would it not be wise of you to give yourself more time and allow God to show you more clearly the rightness or the wrongness of this whole idea? There's so much at stake in the future well-being of both of you."

"Thomas, there's something I haven't told you," Wilberforce admitted. "I already wrote to her, asking for her hand in marriage. The letter is on its way."

"Oh, my goodness, Wilber! You have completely taken leave of your senses! Please, for your sake and mine, as well as Barbara's, go find the letter and hang on to it for at least a few days."

"I think you're wrong about my being too hasty, but I value your judgment and will see if I can intercept the letter. But if not, be assured that I know her to be a great and godly woman, the answer to all my prayers. Waiting for years would not reveal her to be anything other than a wonderful gift of God to me."

William's proposal letter had gone on its way before he could intercept it, and Barbara replied quickly and affirmatively. They had no intention of having a long engagement, but William had to deal with some urgent government business, including clearing himself of some false charges that he had been partly responsible for a mutiny of some sailors. By the end of May, William was able to return to see Barbara, and they were married in a quiet ceremony at the parish church of Walcot in Bath. William's friends set aside their misgivings about the hastiness of the courtship and extended their congratulations and best wishes.

Inevitably, some thought that William could have chosen someone better suited to him and his career. They noted that Barbara was much less outgoing than William, but he liked the fact that she was not interested in the social opportunities open to those prominent in national life. He was much more interested in spending time with those close to him than cultivating political and social opportunities. He had been very close to a number of friends, and now he looked forward to even closer relationships with his own family. Barbara found it hard to adjust to the endless guests and visitors to their house. He loved seeing people but realized that for her sake and for his own health he needed to cut back on some of this social life and the intrusion of political visitors in their home. Barbara's attempts to cut back on his involvement with others was something he understood and accepted. She did not become a great hostess, but he was not particularly concerned about making a great impression, either. He assumed his friends could accept her for who she was, and his deep love for her allowed him to overlook her faults.

In spite of his busy political life, William shared Barbara's desire for a large family, and they began this immediately, having their first two children, William and Barbara, in the first two years after their wedding. God blessed them with three more sons and another daughter. They lived for eleven years in a house at Clapham they bought from Edward Eliot's estate and were able to continue to benefit from the close friendships of that community and the access to political and spiritual counsel. The community valued children, and William enjoyed the time he could spend with their own children, just as he had enjoyed playing with the other children in the community. In 1808 they moved to Kensington to be closer to the House chambers. His departure from Clapham was part of a process in which the community was becoming less lively and beneficial than it had been, but for sixteen years it had everything to do with his spiritual well-being and persistence in his various endeavors.

sixteen

A s far as abolishing the slave trade went, the nineteenth century began as the previous century had ended. Wilberforce remained hopeful and had no intention of giving up. The abolition movement was weak, with Thomas Clarkson no longer actively involved and the Committee for the Abolition of the Slave Trade dormant. William Pitt had been supportive in the early years of the effort, but his backing at the turn of the century seemed doubtful at best. But other events seemed more hopeful. The war with France was looking less threatening. The price of sugar had risen, making the plantation industry determined to protect its supply of cheap labor, but then the price dropped by about half, opening the plantation owners to discussions about ending the slave trade as a means of preventing other nations from gaining an advantage as they expanded their plantations.

While the planters seemed open to discussing the voluntary suspension of the trade for five years, in the final analysis they feared they would never be able to revive the trade after that passage of time. Negotiations with the planters preoccupied Wilberforce during 1800, and he did not introduce an abolition bill in that session. Likewise, in 1801, Wilberforce did not introduce a new bill, instead concentrating on the possibility that peace negotiations with France might open the way for the coordinated ending of the slave trade by both nations. Developments in 1802 and 1803 were no more encouraging. A bill to restrict slave importation to already developed lands was defeated in Commons, and England was preoccupied with the renewal of the war with France in 1803.

Wilberforce and Pitt often discussed political tactics concerning the slave trade. Pitt, always the pragmatist, thought it unwise to push the House of Lords into taking up the bill again.

"Let's assume for the moment that it's not practical or possible to take the abolition bill to the Lords," Wilberforce said to Pitt. "Are there other steps that can be taken?"

"I think the king might be persuaded to enter an Order in Council to stop the slave trade to Dutch Guiana, which we took from Holland during the war. Our planters couldn't object to curtailing the development of this colony. The Dutch will want the colony back after the war, and we could make it a condition of its return that Holland entirely stop its participation in the slave trade."

"I see your point about taking even a small step and doing it by royal proclamation, rather than having it drag on in the Parliament again. This is a matter of international diplomacy and needs an executive action. If you will proceed toward that end, Pitt, I will be grateful."

Pitt and Wilberforce had been able to work together on many political causes, though there were points at which Wilberforce's acts of conscience were a disappointment to Pitt. In this case Wilberforce had reason to be disappointed in Pitt, for Pitt delayed for months the necessary steps to stop the slave trade into Guiana. During this time Pitt became more and more depressed with developments in the war with Napoleon, and illness took its toll on him. In spite of their political differences, Wilberforce remained Pitt's devoted friend and never lost hope that there might be a chance to persuade him that he needed to surrender his soul and his life to Christ. Unfortunately, Bishop Pretyman served as Pitt's spiritual gatekeeper during this final illness, not allowing Wilberforce to come and pray with Pitt for his salvation. Wilberforce was given a prominent place in the funeral procession into Westminster Abbey, but the loss of his friend Pitt and the end of any chance to minister to him spiritually made this a very sad day for Wilberforce.

In a way, Pitt's death became the first step toward the triumph of the abolition cause. Pitt's successor as prime minister was his cousin Lord Grenville, who had joined Pitt in encouraging Wilberforce to take up the slave trade cause in 1787. Grenville remained an ardent supporter of abolition when he assumed office. The Cabinet of the Grenville government included two other strong abolitionists: Charles James Fox, Foreign Secretary, and Lord Henry Petty, Chancellor of the Exchequer. These and other abolitionist voices in the new government outnumbered their opponents on the slave trade question.

James Stephen came to Wilberforce with a new idea. "William, this may sound like heresy, but I've been working with some trusted advisors, and we would like you to hold off for a bit on filing your bill. You're aware that Pitt finally moved ahead on the Order in Council to stop the further importing of slaves to Dutch Guiana. That proclamation needs to be confirmed in Parliament, and this will be seen as very routine. The planters have already given it their support, since they don't want future competition from the Dutch in the Caribbean. So it will be a government bill, and it will move right through the Commons and the Lords. Here's the part that matters. We will ask Grenville to attach your Foreign Slave Bill to the measure, outlawing the carrying of slaves in British ships to any foreign destinations. We will make sure the abolitionists vote for the measure, and we know the government's supporters who are not opposed to slavery will also back the measure."

The first step in the effort to get the abolition bill passed worked as planned. The Dutch Guiana measure passed handily in both houses, seeming to the proslavery interests to be of no significant harm. Behind the scenes, the abolitionists were planning for the second stage. It was May, and Parliament would be adjourning soon, but Wilberforce and Stephen wanted to press on. They concluded that Wilberforce should not be the one to bring the measure to the Commons; Fox would do it there and Grenville would take it to the Lords. Wilberforce reasoned that he probably had made too many enemies along the way, and that two key figures in the new government would be in a stronger position to introduce the measure. He persuaded Grenville and Fox to do their part in this process while he concentrated on composing a plea to the king, calling on him to use the coming peace negotiations as an opportunity to persuade the other European powers to follow England's lead in ending the trade.

In the debate in the Commons, Fox spoke of abolition as an accomplishment that would be well worth his forty years' work in the Parliament. The measure passed easily, and Wilberforce's appeal to the king succeeded as well. As he lay dying that summer, Fox again looked to the hope that the remaining steps toward abolition would be taken soon and expressed pleasure that he had been able to help the cause. In two years, Wilberforce had lost two of the colleagues with whom he had agreed much of the time and with whom he had disagreed a good bit. In both cases, he was sad that they had not found the personal faith in Christ that was so central to his own life.

Even though Grenville had done his part by assuring that the abolition measure passed in the Lords, the session ended without it becoming law. The abolitionists expected this to happen but felt it was important to enter the new session in as strong a position as possible. Between sessions, Grenville called a general election. Wilberforce returned to Yorkshire and campaigned energetically, convincing potential opponents that he had the support of the county. Grenville strengthened his support in the election. Another project for Wilberforce during the recess was the writing of what started out to be a pamphlet and became a full-length book dealing with the slave trade and summarizing all the arguments expressed by the abolitionists during the parliamentary debates. It was his intention to have the book ready for the debate in the next session, and with the heroic efforts of the printer, he nearly accomplished it.

As had been agreed in developing the strategy the summer before, normal practice was to be reversed, and Grenville would introduce the slave trade bill in the Lords first. He would try to head off a request for hearings, but by introducing the bill early in the session there would be time for hearings if they were demanded. When the debate began in the Lords, two events helped build support. Wilberforce's book came out, and news came from the United States that Congress was moving ahead on an abolition bill. Moreover, the abolition committee had come back to life, urging members of Parliament to support the measure.

Grenville presented a strong speech in favor of the measure and ended with a personal tribute to Wilberforce, who was listening in the gallery:

> *I cannot conceive any consciousness more gratifying than must be enjoyed by that person [Wilberforce], on finding a measure to which he has devoted the labor of his life, carried into effect—a measure so truly benevolent, so admirably conducive to the virtuous prosperity of this country, and the welfare of mankind—a measure which will diffuse happiness amongst millions, now in existence, and for which his memory will be blessed by millions yet unborn.*[1]

The vote was surprisingly strong in the Lords, 100 for and 36 against. The remaining steps in the Lords' approval were taken without opposition, clearing the way for prompt action in the Commons. Wilberforce approached this step in the process feeling optimistic but taking nothing for granted. In the past he had brought the measures to the Commons himself, but this time the bill came from the Government with the impetus of its previous passage by the Lords. Soon in the debate it was apparent that the bill would pass. Some opponents rose to speak, but the supporters were more numerous and more forceful. Wilberforce contributed briefly to the discussion, but he could see that the vote would go his way. Sir Samuel Romily echoed Grenville's praise for Wilberforce in the Lords, contrasting the great satisfaction that Wilberforce could take in his accomplishment with the feeling that Napoleon must have had in looking back on the suffering resulting from his conquests:

When he [Wilberforce] compared with these pangs of remorse, the feeling which must accompany his hon. friend from that house to his home, after the vote of that night should have confirmed the object of his humane and unceasing labors; when he should retire into the bosom of his happy and delighted family, when he should lay himself down on his bed, reflecting on the innumerable voices that would be raised in every quarter of the world to bless him; how much more pure and perfect felicity must he enjoy in the consciousness of having preserved so many millions of his fellow-creatures, than the man with whom he had compared him, on the throne to which he had waded

139

through slaughter and oppression.[2]

So dramatically had the pendulum swung in the direction of support for abolition that Romily's moving tribute brought forth an unprecedented standing ovation from House members, with greater force and enthusiasm than could be remembered for any other member. After his twenty years of unrelenting effort, Wilberforce fully deserved the tribute, but he was completely overcome by it. All he could do was sit weeping, thinking back to the time so many years ago he had decided that slavery was one of the causes to which God had called him into public life.

It took another month for the process to be fully completed, including committee action, third reading, confirmation by the Lords, and royal assent. No one doubted the outcome during that stage, but Wilberforce breathed more freely when all these steps had been completed.

"William," Thornton asked, "how do you feel now that you've finished what you set out to do?"

"Henry, I feel a lot of relief and gratitude to God, but we haven't finished much at all. If we could have ended slavery entirely and emancipated the slaves in the empire, that would have been an accomplishment. I have every intention of going to work immediately to tackle the slavery problem. Righteousness will conquer evil. God will defeat the enemies. Some day we will have another celebration. If I'm in heaven then, there will be a huge chorus of angels at my side, rejoicing when the slaves are free."

seventeen

Wilberforce had been thinking about the Sierra Leone colony, which he and Henry Thornton had actively supported over the years. Now that the slave trade had ended, he thought it would be appropriate for Sierra Leone to become an official British colony. That would facilitate the use of Freetown as a staging area for the navy in patrolling the coast to look for British ships whose owners might think they were not serious about the slave trade law.

Wilberforce had already set things in motion for a public meeting to promote the founding of an "African Institute" whose goals would be the promotion of the civilization and improvement of all of Africa. He had talked with the duke of Gloucester about hosting a meeting in the Freemasons' Hall to which they would invite many

141

national leaders. Wilberforce believed the time was right to direct their energies to something immediately impacting the great continent of Africa.

Thornton agreed that the time was right to promote this more ambitious effort in Africa. They needed something more comprehensive than what they had been able to do in Sierra Leone. New and constructive openings for trade with Africa were needed, along with more opportunities for those Africans who chose to return to their homeland.

Four years after the passage of the slave trade bill and the founding of the African Institute, Wilberforce paced back and forth in his room, pausing sometimes to drop to his knees in prayer, at other times to laboriously list the pros and cons of the decision he was facing. Thirty-one years ago he had been elected to Parliament, and now he faced a momentous choice. He saw three possibilities: continuing his increasingly burdensome duties as they were, dropping out of the Commons entirely, or resigning from his seat representing Yorkshire to seek a small borough with fewer demands on his time.

Wilberforce talked with his Christian friends about the decision and found no clear agreement among them. Some could see that his health was declining and counseled him to leave politics entirely. His colitis continued with little relief, and he had to maintain his regular doses of opium. He was also suffering from the early stages of curvature of the spine, and before long would experience the annoying necessity of wearing a cumbersome leather brace with steel stays. One shoulder had begun to sag, and without determined effort, his head fell forward against his chest.

Also weighing on the side of leaving politics were the

challenges of being a good father to six children, the oldest of which was then thirteen. He and Barbara had a number of governesses and tutors, but Wilberforce was not comfortable with the common practice among the wealthy of delegating the entire raising of children to their domestic staff. He loved reading to the children, playing games with them, and spending time with them, even when they tended toward being out of control. During the busy times of Parliament's session, he found it very hard to spend much time with them. One incident that pushed him toward cutting back on his duties was the time one of his sons began crying when he picked him up. "He always is afraid of strangers," said the child's nurse, filling Wilberforce with guilt and sadness.[1]

Occasionally a constituent from Yorkshire would complain when Wilberforce did not respond to a letter on a timely basis. No matter how hard he tried, he could not keep up with his correspondence, nor could he find time to see everyone who came to him with requests and complaints. He had fought for twenty years for the passage of the slave trade bill, had worked on numerous projects such as the Sierra Leone colony, and was visibly exhausted.

In making his decision, Wilberforce was probably influenced by the needs of his family as much as anything. As he prayed and journaled, his responsibility for his children's moral training weighed heavily on him. He wrote in his journal, "They claim a father's heart, eye, and voice, and friendly intercourse. Now so long as I am M.P. for Yorkshire, it will, I fear, be impossible for me to give my heart and time to the work as I ought, unless I become a negligent M.P. such as does not become our great country."[2] Adding to his concern

143

for the children was Barbara's longstanding anxiety about his health and the stress his public life placed on the family.

Wilberforce took the middle ground in this hard decision, deciding to resign the Yorkshire seat and accept the offer of representing the small borough of Bramber in Sussex. Barbara's cousin, Lord Calthorpe, controlled the borough and was an admirer of Wilberforce. He was pleased to have William accept appointment from Bramber. This was not an easy thing for a person who had always supported the need for reform in an electoral system that made possible exactly the kind of "pocket borough" he was going to represent. Unlike William Pitt, who had entered Parliament from a pocket borough at the very beginning, Wilberforce had taken the high road in winning elections with legitimate campaigns. He struggled with the inconsistencies involved in the decision but took the pragmatic approach that he could still support parliamentary reform while availing himself of the opportunity to continue his career without the enormous demands of a huge constituency.

Wilberforce made another decision that was intended to increase the time he could spend with his family, although it didn't have that effect immediately. They moved to a house in Kensington, a mile from the parliamentary buildings. This decreased his commute time but increased the problem of constituents showing up at his house asking for help of various sorts. Wilberforce loved to be with people and tolerated the chaos that resulted from their many visitors until he resigned from the Yorkshire seat.

William and Barbara's devotion to their children was amply rewarded by the success of three of their four sons, who each went to the strongest college at Oxford, earned honors, and took up careers as clergymen. They applied themselves in ways that William wished he had done at Cambridge. But the pathway of their oldest son, William, was quite a different matter. In his early years in school he did not apply himself and sometimes acted in immature ways. At Cambridge young William was even less diligent in his studies than his father had been. He spent money wastefully, lied to his parents, and disgraced them by getting drunk after his friend died and was awaiting burial. The elder William blamed himself for his son's waywardness, writing in his journal,

> *O my poor William. How strange he can make so miserable those who love him best and whom really he loves. His soft nature makes him the sport of his companions, and the wicked and idle naturally attach themselves like dust and cleave like burrs. I go to pray for him. Alas, could I love my Savior more and serve Him, God would hear my prayer and turn his heart. . . .[3]*

Wilberforce's agonized prayers for his eldest son were answered in the sense that their relationship remained strong, and young William did not become completely prodigal. The elder William felt he must remove his son from Cambridge until he became more serious about his studies, but he never returned to the university. He undertook legal studies with a friend of his father but did not do well there, either.

In the nine years he represented the Bramber borough,

145

Wilberforce was able to slow his pace somewhat because of the reduced demands from constituents, but he continued with a variety of causes on the floor of Commons. He worked unsuccessfully to eliminate the ban on Catholics serving in the House of Commons. He was successful in his campaign to allow Christian missionaries to be admitted to service in India. He was unsuccessful in bringing about England's recognition of Haiti but provided encouragement and assistance to King Christophe of the new republic of Haiti.

While he worked on these and other causes in Parliament, Wilberforce's passion continued to be the emancipation of the slaves in England's colonies and, if possible, in all European colonies. He tried two strategies, neither of which was successful, but both of which helped keep the issue alive. One was the effort to require that a register of slaves be kept by colonial administrators. This was meant to assist in documenting the illegal importation of slaves. The slave interests in the colonies opposed this effort in Parliament. Later the colonial legislatures passed measures requiring that registers of slaves be kept, but the legislators passed these bills with no intention of implementing them.

Wilberforce and his allies in the emancipation effort also worked on the diplomatic front, lobbying participants in the European peacemaking conferences to include a provision in the treaty ending the Napoleonic wars that would ban any European participation in the slave trade. Nothing was accomplished at first, but then Napoleon returned to take power again in France and abolished the slave trade in the French empire in an effort to win support from

England. When Louis XVIII was restored to the throne of France, he confirmed Napoleon's abolition decree, and an abolition provision was added to the treaties coming from the Congress of Vienna. Things are not always as they seem, however, for none of the eight participants in the peace discussions, except England, made any effort to stop the slave trade.

The failure of these efforts strengthened the determination of the antislavery forces in England to press for the goal they would have desired from the beginning, the complete emancipation of slaves in the British Empire. But Wilberforce was experiencing more frequent health problems, and it became apparent to him that he must find someone younger to carry on the work in the Parliament. Many of the abolition core group from Clapham were no longer alive. Henry Thornton had died in 1815. There was no one in sight to take over from Wilberforce until he met Thomas Buxton, who won election to the Commons in 1818. The two men were from merchant families, and both were committed evangelicals. Buxton took up causes that connected well with the values of Wilberforce, including prison reform, the improvement of working conditions in industry, and the abolition of the death penalty. Buxton had numerous connections with the Quakers, who had been consistent backers of abolition and emancipation. Buxton's sister-in-law, Elizabeth Fry, was a strong leader in prison reform.

Wilberforce discussed his problems with Buxton. "I may have to retire from Parliament before long, and I would like to start working with someone from within the Commons who would take up the cause. There are still plenty of people working behind the scenes, but someone will be needed in Parliament to take the lead, just as I attempted to do with the abolition effort more than thirty years ago. Thomas, I'm asking you to consider being that person."

"I'm sure you realize I'm not nearly as well versed on the slavery issue as I am regarding some of the other causes I've taken up. I honestly don't know if I'm the one to take up your mantle, but believe me, I'm deeply touched that you've asked me. I certainly can't give you an immediate answer. All I can say is that I will pray carefully about it. I will not agree to do it unless I'm sure God wants me to do this, and that I can give it my complete energy. Please pray that I will be led to the right decision."

Wilberforce was not idle while Buxton made up his mind about taking over the leadership of the emancipation effort in Parliament. In early 1823, Wilberforce helped organize a large rally to bring into being the Anti-Slavery Society, the goal of which was to generate popular support for the complete emancipation of the slaves. Wilberforce wrote a pamphlet in support of emancipation and presented a petition calling on Parliament to abolish slavery.

After some months of thought and prayer, Buxton agreed to take up Wilberforce's work on emancipation. That opened the way for Wilberforce to begin making a graceful exit from the national political stage. In remarks to the Anti-Slavery Society in mid-1824, he gave a sort of benediction to his work:

We have been engaged in many a long and
arduous contest, and we also have had to contend

with calumny and falsehood. But we are more than repaid, by the success that has already attended our efforts, and by the anticipations which we may derive from what we have witnessed this very day, when, if our sun be setting, we see that other luminaries are arising to shine with far greater lustre and more efficient strength.[4]

eighteen

uxton, my health this year has gotten decidedly worse, and sometimes I just do not have the strength to do the very few things I need to do in the Parliament. Thomas, what I'm saying is that I'm about to resign from Parliament, and I wanted you to be the first to know."

Buxton reminded Wilberforce that the antislavery forces still needed his courageous spirit and the great respect he had in Commons and among the people. There would be times they needed him to stand up and use his incomparable powers of persuasion.

Wilberforce could not be moved. If it really were true that things could not go forward without him, he would be very sad indeed, for his body could no longer keep up with his spirit. In a short amount of time, Buxton had shown himself to be a good choice to carry the cause of emancipation in the Commons. "I may not live to see the final conquest, but God's righteousness will be restored in our land, at least in this respect. I have no doubt of that."

Had Wilberforce felt free to completely follow his wife's preferences, he would have stepped down long ago. She felt it her duty to protect him from further physical suffering and an untimely death. Now he could see that his ailments were causing her anxiety, and though he could continue to endure some suffering himself, he did not want to bring more on her.

"Our worth as Christians is not in our power and prestige, Buxton, but in our relationship with the heavenly Father. When we feel led to pass our work on to others, we can be sure that the same God who called us to this work will raise up others to carry it on. I'm delighted that you have accepted part of the work, and there are many others who will help. As a follower of Christ, I can trust the work of the kingdom of God will get done in God's time. My time in this work has come and gone, and I must say I have great peace about laying aside the office I hold and giving myself more diligently to my family and other causes."

Wilberforce had earned the quieter life in which he was now able to engage. He established a routine of daily prayers, hearing his correspondence read, conversing with family and friends, and answering his letters. He was able to enjoy the accomplishments of his children, although he had to continue struggling with the misfortunes of his oldest son, William. Young William studied for the bar but abandoned his studies when ill health hindered his diligence. With major financial backing from his father and loans from numerous others, young William bought a dairy farm and a retail milk business. It had the potential to support his family, but in a short time the business had failed and the debts had multiplied.

Young William headed for Europe to get away from his creditors. His father could have left it to others to deal with his son but felt compelled to take full responsibility for the debts. He sold the farm he had bought when they left London, plus the family lands in Yorkshire, leaving him with no home and very little income. He made a virtue from a necessity, however, professing to enjoy the simplification of his life and the chance to spend time with each of their children.

In the late 1820s and early 1830s, Buxton and the emancipation group in Parliament continued their efforts with little to show for it. Nevertheless, popular support continued to grow, as evidenced by the turnout of two thousand people at the 1830 Anti-Slavery meeting. Wilberforce participated in this rally, though he was physically weak. Three years later he made his last public appearance, speaking out once again in support of emancipation. He was extremely frail but reached deep inside for some of the passion that had always characterized his work on behalf of the slaves.

"You look like a man with a mission, Macaulay. Are you the bearer of good news or bad news, my friend?"

"Decidedly good news, Mr. Wilberforce. The victory is ours. Yesterday the House passed on second reading the measure to abolish slavery. The Lords will certainly concur, and the king will agree to the measure. At last the day has come."

"It has indeed. This great news has preceded you, Macaulay, and I have not stopped thanking the Lord since I heard it. Some folks spend their whole lives working toward some important end and are not blessed to see its accomplishment. That to which I committed my life almost half a century ago has now come about. I am so blessed to see this day. Not only has the end of slavery come about, but our government has agreed to dip into the treasury to assure that the slave owners have the money to seek some more honorable economic pursuits. Should it be the desire of my heavenly Father to take me home shortly, I shall go with great rejoicing."

The time between that conversation with Thomas Macaulay and Wilberforce's death was only a matter of hours. Shortly after his death, his widow Barbara expressed the kind of perspective on his death consistent with her husband's great trust in God and certainty of eternal life:

> *Why should I wish to detain in a sinking, ema-ciated suffering body, such a spirit from eternal joys, from a state where pain and sorrow and above all sin, are to be known no more? My loss is indeed beyond measure and expression great, but to him, I trust, it is unspeakable gain and I ought to be full of thankfulness that such a trea-sure was spared to me, to his family, to his coun-try, and to the world so long, and recalled at last with so little comparative suffering, especially of acute pain, which the exquisite sensibility of his delicate frame so little enabled him to cope with.*[1]

On the statue of William Wilberforce in Westminster Abbey, where he was buried, are these words:

> *In an age and country fertile in great and good men, he was among the foremost of those who fixed the character of their times because to high and various talents, to warm benevolence, and to universal candor, he added the abiding eloquence of a Christian life.*[2]

The word suggested by this epitaph and by William Wilberforce's entire life is *extraordinary*. In no way does it exaggerate the significance of his life to connect this word with the high points of who he was and what he accomplished:

EXTRAORDINARY SPIRITUAL REBIRTH—
Wilberforce was an undisciplined, spoiled rich child who did only enough during his years in school and at Cambridge University to get by and graduate. He reached his goals of having a good time and making friends. Within a few years, he found his way out of the emptiness of his life into a transforming experience with Jesus Christ as Savior and Lord. He never stopped being witty and personable, but his life took on a seriousness and dedication he had never experienced before. He was a very different man, and his spiritual life became the single most important part of who he was from that time forward.

EXTRAORDINARY FOCUS—Wilberforce entered politics for lack of anything better to do. He had no goals, no passion, and no issues. After he committed his life to Christ, he sought a purpose in politics and found it in his goals of transforming British moral conduct and bringing an end to the single greatest human evil of the day, slavery. He became involved with many issues and projects in his career, but from beginning to end he remained focused on moral reform and emancipation.

EXTRAORDINARY ELECTORAL SUCCESS—When Wilberforce made the giant leap from representing Hull to winning the most prestigious seat in the Commons, representing Yorkshire, he did so with very little apparent forethought or plan. But he had charisma, great oratorical skill, and superb timing. His success in winning the seat and holding it through-out his battle against slavery was extremely important in providing him political longevity and power.

EXTRAORDINARY IMPACT ON HUMAN BEHAVIOR— Wilberforce never intended to limit his efforts to the slavery problem. His very early conviction was that God had also called him to work in the private sector, through such channels as the Proclamation Societies, to turn people toward more honest and upright living. He and his fellow believers in the Parliament and other leadership positions continued to set a strong example of integrity and godly living.

EXTRAORDINARY DETERMINATION TO ELIMI-NATE SLAVERY—Twenty years is a very long time to work on one issue, especially when it was apparent to most abolitionists that their real goal was emanci-pation. The number of defeats in Parliament toward the goal reached in 1807 are almost too many to count. For Wilberforce to achieve the abolition victory and then begin immediately to work on emancipation is most amazing. He had no way of knowing the second goal would take another twenty-six years, but in a way it didn't matter to Wilberforce. He was convinced it was essential to reach the goal and had no thought of giving up.

EXTRAORDINARY IMPACT OF HIS BOOK—
Politicians and other activists don't often have time to write books, much less to write good and successful books. Wilberforce's book on Christian living had a huge impact on his contemporaries and still is a useful guide to Christian conduct. He applied the same determination in getting the book done that he did in pursuing political goals. He had very little time to write, but he got it done, and a whole generation was influenced by it.

EXTRAORDINARY SURVIVAL PHYSICALLY—
Wilberforce's illnesses as a young man made it appear that he would not live long, especially since the doctors had only a vague notion of the source of his pain. The doctors prescribed opium, and with God's help and his own self-discipline, he was able to avoid becoming addicted to the drug and continued its daily use to control his digestive ailments. He outlived many of his contemporaries in spite of the stressful life he lived. He was a walking example of God's grace and healing.

EXTRAORDINARY DIVERSITY OF INTERESTS—
Wilberforce is primarily remembered for his work

against slavery, but his involvement in other causes was almost limitless, inside and outside the government. He sought to help the victims of society—the orphans, single mothers, and chimney sweeps. He was active in a long list of Christian groups, including the Society for Bettering the Cause of the Poor, the Church Missionary Society, the British and Foreign Bible Society, the African Institute, and the Anti-Slavery Society. Someone attempted to count the charitable groups he assisted with his efforts and his philanthropy and came up with a list of sixty-nine groups.

EXTRAORDINARY DEATH—To be lucid and personable two days before he died was an amazing gift for a person who endured many physical problems. God honored Wilberforce's faithfulness and determination by allowing him to live until Parliament had voted on the emancipation bill and it was certain to pass. His work of fifty years was accomplished, and he could go to meet Jesus with a keen sense of "the abiding eloquence of a Christian life."

appendix

The following is the final chapter of William Wilberforce's book The Practical View of the Prevailing Religious System of Professed Christians in the Higher and Middle Classes of This Country Contrasted with Real Christianity. *In it, Wilberforce offers "Practical Hints to Different Sorts of People." The text has been lightly edited and modernized by Ellyn Sanna.*

Some of Our Most Common Self-Deceptions

Throughout this book I have been trying to outline the main problems with the religious systems of most professed Christians in this country. I have pointed out their meager concept of the importance of Christianity in general, their inadequate understanding of its most important doctrines, and the effect that all of this produces on everyday morals, causing their strictness to be relaxed. Most of all, I have shown how mistaken many of us are about Christianity's true essence.

After saying all this, I hope that no one will think that the differences between nominal Christians and true believers are so minor that they count for very little, as though they were merely superficial differences that had to

159

do with exterior forms and practices. The very substance of our faith is in question; the difference between real faith and that which is only nominal is serious and momentous.

We must speak out. Their Christianity is not real Christianity. It lacks the radical interior principle of Christ. It is defective in all its most important aspects. Those who follow this counterfeit system must no longer deceive themselves with words and language; no matter what they may call themselves, they are not true followers of Christ. This matter is too important for anyone to mistake its real nature. With humble prayers to the source of all wisdom, that He would enlighten their understanding and clear their hearts from prejudice, these people must seriously examine their beliefs and practices, using the Scripture as their standard. If they do so, they will become aware of the shallowness of their inadequate system of belief.

If through God's blessing on anything I have written, people should become inspired to look at themselves, seriously examining their lives and their beliefs, then let me warn them right now that all of us are prone to thinking too favorably of ourselves. Selfishness is one of the principal fruits of human corruption, and obviously, selfishness disposes us to overrate our good qualities, while we overlook or excuse our faults. If we acknowledge the corruption of human nature, then it follows undeniably that in all our self-examination, if we want to form an accurate estimate of our character, we must make allowance for the effects of selfishness.

Another effect of human corruption is that it clouds our moral vision and blunts our moral sensitivity. We have to allow for this effect, as well. Without a doubt, God's perfect purity allows Him to see in us far more stains than we can see; what is more, in His eyes they look larger and blacker than we can perceive. Nor should we forget another awful consideration: When we look at ourselves, we are most apt to have a deep impression of only our most recent and obvious sins. Many individual acts of selfishness—or even a continued course of destructive and selfish behavior—smite us with remorse when we first commit them, but as the months and years go by, we forget our shame. Time numbs our conscience, and our memories retain only a faint trace of our sins. But we can only determine the true measure of our guilt by looking at our strongest impressions of the selfish things we have done, not by surveying the faded images that time has left us.

Even then, to God's pure eyes, this guilt will always appear far greater than it does to us. For Him there is no past or future; whatever has been is retained in His mind with eternal and unchanging endurance, just as though it had first happened. This is yet another reason why He perceives our sin so much more clearly than we ever can with our limited minds. Such thoughts should humble us in God's sight, for unless our offenses have been blotted out by Christ, through our true repentance and living faith, we will appear before God clothed in the sins of an entire lifetime. We may no longer particularly remember the circumstances of these sins—we may only have a vague recollection of shame and embarrassment—but God will see them in all their original depth of coloring. I am telling you all this from personal experience. I have found that no other thoughts than the ones I am describing are quite so effective in helping me humble myself before God's mercy, aware of my true condition of need and imperfection.

While we are talking about some of the mistaken ways we judge our spiritual and moral character, this might be a good time to point out some other all too common sources of self-deception. Many people, as we implied earlier, are misled by the favorable opinions that others have of them; many others, I am afraid, mistake in themselves a hot zeal for orthodoxy, that heartfelt acceptance of the gospel's great truths that is so necessary to our spiritual health; and almost all of us, at one time or another, are confused to one degree or another by the fact that intellectually we give our support to some doctrine, while it fails to touch our hearts or conduct. A cold head knowledge is not the same as a sincere and deep conviction of the heart. Knowing something intellectually is never enough to lead us to the intense determination to change our lives that is so necessary to repentance.

I don't want to fail to mention another source of self-deception, a dangerous and harmful one that is all too common. In order to explain what I am talking about better, let me say first that certain selfish habits and also certain good qualities seem to come more naturally when we experience particular periods or conditions in our lives. Given that, if we would want to accurately assess our spiritual and moral condition, we need to examine ourselves in reference to that particular "sin which does most easily beset us"; we should not base our determination on some other sin to which we are not particularly liable, at least for now. In the same way, on the other hand, we shouldn't pat ourselves on the backs if we find in ourselves some good and pleasant quality that comes to us naturally at this point in our lives. Instead, we need to look for some less ambiguous sign that faith is alive and real within our hearts, a controlling principle of goodness in all we do. Instead, though, we are apt to reverse these rules: We are likely, on the one hand—both with ourselves and with others—to excuse "the besetting sin," considering that we should all be exempt from the guilt of something to which we are so prone—and on the other hand, we tend to take great pride in the fact that we possess some sweet and good quality, even though it comes to us naturally, requiring no moral effort on our part. The bad effects of this tendency are only aggravated by the practice—to which we are all sadly prone—of being contented with a hasty view of ourselves. We accept negative evidence—we are not shocked by some enormous and outright sin, and so, since we lack this obvious problem, we assume we are in good condition—rather than looking for positive proofs that we are true Christians, the sort of proof that is spelled out in Scripture.

But the source of self-deception that I am most concerned about here is found in our tendency to consider that we have conquered a particular sin because we have changed the circumstances of our lives. In other words, as we grow older we leave behind the conditions that made us once so susceptible to one sort of temptation. But that does not mean that we don't substitute another form of self-ishness in place of the one that so controlled us when we were younger. Each age and circumstance of our lives have their own temptations. We cannot take pride in the fact that we outgrow some sins, or give them up merely because of some change in our external circumstances. This proves nothing about the internal state of our hearts.

This topic deserves to be examined a little more closely. Young people are very likely to be inconsiderate and controlled by their bodies; male youths in particular suffer great physical temptations, and female young people are just as tempted by physical appearances and empty pleasures. These temptations come naturally to them; neither of these tendencies prove that the young people in question are particularly sinful or evil. Provided that they are good-natured and open and not disobedient to their parents or others in authority, we usually think of them as good-hearted young men and innocent young women. Those who love them best aren't worried about their spiritual interests, and we all assume that as these young people grow older, they will naturally become more serious and interested in spiritual concerns. We don't think that God is upset with them, nor do we consider them to be in any real danger. We assume that in the end they will turn out all right.

These young people grow older and marry. The same tendency to sexual sin that we accepted in a teenage boy, we now regard in a husband and a father as being incompatible with the character of a decent and good man. We say something like this: "He has sown his wild oats. Now it's time for him to mend his ways and settle down." We have the same feeling about the married woman; she should no longer be so totally concerned with her physical appearance and having a good time. However, if these people now become good and loving spouses and parents, if their behavior conforms to our expectations of them, then we all assume that they are a very good sort of people. We have no worries that they are in any eternal danger, and we are happy that they have become such respectable members of society.

In reality, however, these people were never much concerned with spiritual matters, and while their external lives appear settled and happy, they still have no interest in a life of faith. They have no interest in the great work of their salvation, for they are preoccupied with earning money and raising their families. Meanwhile, they congratulate themselves on becoming so righteous, for they no longer commit the sins of their youth. In reality, however, they're not even tempted to commit these sins anymore, so how can their abstinence be considered any test of their moral characters? On top of that, if they were to commit the sins of their youth, they would likely be censured by society. That sort of selfish behavior could easily make them lose the things they are most concerned with now, and so they refrain from these behaviors, not out of any sense of spiritual morality, but because it is to their own best interests to do so.

Eventually, these same people will grow old. Now, if ever, we might expect that they would begin to think about eternal things. No such thing! They are still pleasant people. We see in them an appropriate measure of peace, and so we are not worried about them. They have no worries for themselves, either, for they are quite satisfied with their characters. We expect them now to be good-natured and cheerful, indulgent of the frailties and foolishness of young people, remembering that when they were young themselves, they, too, gave in to the same practices.

The true Christian, however, has a dread of sin. She would never smile at watching some young person commit the same sin that once tempted her. She can only look back on the sins of her younger days with shame and sorrow. Her past experiences prompt her to warn young people about their lives. But we see none of these qualities in the imaginary people we have followed through their lives. Throughout their entire lifetimes, they have found some means or other to stifle the voices of their consciences. We might say of them that they "cry peace while there is no peace." And yet none of us worry about them. We all judge each other and ourselves by external appearances rather than on our consciousness that we are reconciled with God through Christ.

Some readers may feel I am being harsh and judgmental in what I have just said. I am sorry, but I cannot be deterred by fears that others will think I am being unloving. It is time to be done with all this senseless talk of love, for it insults our intelligence, and it trifles with the sincere feelings of those who are truly concerned with the happiness of their fellow creatures. Those of us who are taken in by this false thinking are only storing up remorse and bitter self-reproaches for our future torment. We who have the responsibility of watching over the eternal interests of our children and friends are allowing ourselves to be lulled asleep, beguiled by this sort of shallow reasoning that convinces us to spare ourselves the momentary pain of carrying out our important duties!

True love is in fact partial to the loved one, and this partiality makes us more inclined to credit our loved ones with good motives rather than bad ones. We are apt also to exaggerate our loved one's good qualities and to see them in a more favorable light than they may strictly deserve. But true love is also alert, fervent, full of concern and the desire to do that which is best for the loved one. It is not so easily satisfied, not so ready to believe that everything is going well as a matter of course; it is on its guard against dangers, and it is prompt to offer help and protection. These are the symptoms by which we recognize the genuine love of a wife or a mother; we would expect her to take good care to ensure that her family is physically healthy, rather than looking the other way when illness or danger threatens her loved ones—and she should show the same concern for their spiritual interests. We all should, if we say that we love each other. Too often what we call love today is really only selfish indifference. We cannot be bothered by the needs of others; we would rather assume that everything is fine than feel anxious or fearful about those for whom we care. We want to be happy all the time, our peace undisturbed. Real love, however, often goes up and down emotionally. It is flushed with hope one moment and chilled by disappointment another.

If you are truly a thoughtful person, one who is aware of the spiritual world around us, you will be concerned when you see thoughtless parents delighted by their young people's engaging cheerfulness and cloudless high spirits. These parents feel no concern for their children's spiritual well-being; they assume that their children's youthful qualities are sufficient proof of their spiritual purity. Youth, however, gives us opportunities that we can never reexperience. It would be a shame for our young people not to take advantage of this period when they are forming their spiritual habits for a lifetime. This is the time to shape in them the ways of thinking that will be of most use to them as they grow more mature. If they are going to be ready to teach children of their own, they must begin to learn spiritual wisdom now, when they have the time.

Can you think of a more pleasing image than that of a couple who are happy with each other and with the pledges of their mutual love, united together in grateful adoration of God, the author of all their joys? Their prayers for each other, their love and parental tenderness, their confidence that God will work all the changes in their lives together for the good of those who love and put their trust in Him, their hope that they will one day come together into a state of never-ending happiness; all these are some of the most moving expressions of God's grace that we will ever see.

Both man and woman have their own parts to play in bringing faith to the next generation, and the woman's role is particularly important. How can we ever think that the female sex is inferior when we see the essential responsibility God has given women in this world? Their sensitivity to spiritual concerns seems to be far more innate and natural than a man's. Mothers and wives often are the medium for our intercourse with the heavenly world, the faithful repositories of spiritual knowledge and wisdom. We should all be careful to avail ourselves of the benefits they have to offer both the present generation and the one that will follow us. And we should be saddened whenever we see our world today encouraging women to settle for something less than the true calling God has given them. The world would like to hand women an empty package, one that looks pretty on the outside but that contains nothing but empty dissipation and selfish pleasures. We demean women when we lend our support to the image of womanhood that has become fashionable in today's world, especially among the upper classes.

Innocent young women! Good-hearted young men! What is this goodness of heart and this innocence based on? Remember that we are all fallen creatures, born to sin and naturally depraved. Christianity recognizes no natural innocence or goodness of heart; our only innocence and goodness come from the remission of sin through Christ, the effects of divine grace. Do we see in these young people the sort of characters that the Bible describes as the only satisfactory evidence of eternal safety? Or do we see instead qualities that tell of a state of alienation from God? No matter how much we may love these young people, can we really persuade ourselves that they know anything about real love for others? Does anything indicate that they are striving "to love God with all their hearts, and minds, and souls, and strength"? Are they "seeking first the kingdom of God, and his righteousness"? Are they "working out their salvation with fear and trembling"? Are they "clothed with humility"? Aren't they instead totally devoted to self-indulgence? At the very least, can't we see that they are "lovers of pleasure more than lovers of God"? Do they find comfort in spiritual activities? Or do they come to sacred services with reluctance; do they attend only because they are made to by their parents, and are they relieved to be done with them? Are we forced to say of these young people that "The harp, and the viol, the tabret, and pipe, and wine, are in their feasts: but they regard not the work of the LORD, neither consider the operation of his hands" (Isa. 5:12)? Is not this young man obsessed with thinking about a certain sort of sin, even if he never actually commits it (and more than likely he does), even though this is a sin of which the Bible says expressly, "that they which do such things shall not inherit the kingdom of God"? Isn't this young woman preoccupied with gratifying her vanity, finding her source of all happiness in fashion and parties and the admiration of others?

And then, when youths' high spirits are over, what does their so-called reformation really mean? They may be decent, sober, useful, respectable members of the community, good-natured and responsible in their homes. But is this the change of which the Scripture speaks? Listen to the phrases the Bible uses and judge for yourselves: "Except a man be born again, he cannot see the kingdom of God" (John 3:3); "The old man. . .is corrupt according to the deceitful lusts" (Eph. 4:22) (an expression that is all too descriptive of youth's selfish delirium and the false dreams of pleasure that it inspires). But "the new man" has woken up to the truth about this false thinking; he is "renewed in knowledge after the image of him that created him" (Col. 3:10); he "after God is created in righteousness and true holiness" (Eph. 4:24).

As they grow older, the people of whom we have been speaking are no longer so thoughtless and wild and dissipated as before. They are no longer so negligent of the things that really matter, nor do they pursue their own pleasures so eagerly. Neither are they as prone to yield to the impulses of their physical appetites. But this is no more than a natural change that happens to almost everyone.

This is a point of infinite importance. Don't think I am being tedious by spending so long on it. In fact, I want to take the opportunity to discuss this matter a little more. With that goal in sight, let me ask another question that will help readers judge whether I am being too harsh—or whether in fact I am making an accurate portrayal of the truth.

Are we passing the test that God has put before us? A test of this nature implies that if we follow God's will in our lives, we must resist a temptation that we are naturally prompted to gratify. Young people are not normally tempted to be greedy, critical, or harsh-spoken. Instead, they are far more apt to be thoughtless of the feelings of others, while they yield to their own physical temptations; they tend to be "lovers of pleasure more than lovers of God." Middle-aged people, on the other hand, are not so strongly tempted to be thoughtless and lazy and licentious. Family responsibilities, social connections, and tradition are enough to restrain them from these sort of excesses. Older people, however, must face another test. They are tempted to be obsessed with worldly cares, with their family's interests, with professional goals, with the pursuit of wealth or ambition. Thus occupied, they are tempted to "mind earthly rather than heavenly things," forgetting "the one thing needful"; they are likely to "set their affections" on earthly rather than eternal concerns. They take "a form of godliness" instead of seeking to experience the power of Christ in their lives; they forget—or they are totally ignorant of, as I have already said—the real doctrines of their faith.

These are the ready-made Christians that I have mentioned before, those who consider Christianity to be a geographical term that applies to anyone who was born and educated in a country where Christianity is professed. They do not understand that a real Christian is someone who has a renewed nature and a unique character, nor do they comprehend that Christianity carries with it its own collection of desires and aversions, hopes and fears, joys and sorrows. Christ said to these people, "I know thy works, that thou hast a name that thou livest, and art dead. Be watchful, and strengthen the things which remain, that are ready to die: for I have not found thy works perfect before God. Remember therefore how thou hast received and heard, and hold fast, and repent. If therefore thou shalt not watch, I will come on thee as a thief, and thou shalt not know what hour

I will come upon thee" (Rev. 3:1–3).

If any of my readers are inclined to listen to this solemn warning, if any of you have been awakened from your dreams of false security, if you are ready now to be not only an almost Christian but an entire one—oh, please don't stifle this dawning sense of the seriousness of your condition. Instead, carefully cherish these new thoughts as the "workings of the Holy Spirit" that will draw you from the "broad and crowded" road of destruction into that narrow path "that leadeth to life." Go away by yourself for awhile; spend some time alone in prayer. On bended knees, implore Christ, relying on His mediation, to "take away from you the heart of stone, and give you a heart of flesh." Ask the Father of light to open your eyes to your true condition, and clear the clouds of prejudice from your heart. Plead with Him to erase the lies of self-love. Then carefully examine your past life and your present course of action, comparing yourself with God's Word. Consider how your actions look in light of the Bible's words. If you acknowledge Scripture to be the revelation of the will of your creator and supreme gift-giver, then read what the Bible has to say about sinners who do not repent. Try to become more and more deeply impressed with a sense of your own desperate blindness and corruption.

And above all, steadily contemplate this one stupendous truth: The only begotten Son of God became a human being and was crucified for us. Listen to the message of mercy that Jesus proclaimed from the cross to all sinners who repent: "Be ye reconciled unto God"; "Believe in the Lord Jesus Christ, and thou shalt be saved."

When you have an accurate picture of your guilt after looking at the high price that was required to atone for it—

and at the same, when you comprehend how much your soul must be worth to Jesus—if your heart hasn't become numb and cold, you will surely be nearly overwhelmed with mixed emotions of guilt and fear, shame and remorse and sorrow. When you think how rude and inconsiderate you have been toward God, and you reflect on the amazing love and compassion of Christ, you will hit yourself on your breast and cry out in the words of the publican, "God be merciful to me a sinner." Think about the cold and formal acknowledgment that up until now you have given this being who loves you so much; remember how you have undervalued the precious blood of the Son of God and have trifled with the gracious invitations of your redeemer—and you will be overcome with remorse.

But blessed be God! You do not need to despair. Jesus offers the gospel to people who are just like you, in the very condition where you find yourself. The gospel's promises are for those who are "weary and heavy-laden" under the burden of their sins, to those who thirst for the water of life, to those who feel themselves "tied and bound by the chain of their sins," who abhor their captivity and long for deliverance. Be happy! The grace of God has visited you and "has brought you out of darkness into his marvellous light," "from the power of Satan unto God."

Throw yourself completely then on His undeserved mercy. He is full of love, and He will never reject you. Surrender yourselves into His hands and solemnly resolve, through His grace, to dedicate from now on all your abilities and powers to His service.

Your job now is "to work out your own salvation with fear and trembling," relying on the faithfulness of Him who has promised to "work in you both to will and to do of his good pleasure." Look to Him for help all the time; your only safety consists in a deep and abiding sense of your own weakness and a firm reliance on His strength. If you "give all diligence" to keeping close to Jesus, His power will be there for your protection; His truth is pledged for your security. You are enlisted under the banner of Christ—so fear not, even though the world and the flesh and the devil are all ready to fight against you. "Faithful is he that hath promised"; "be ye also faithful unto death, and he will give you a crown of life"; "he that endureth to the end, the same shall be saved."

In the world we live in, in the society we live in, especially if we have power and affluence, you must be prepared to meet with many difficulties; so be prepared. Arm yourself with a determined resolution to never rate human approval beyond its true value, nor to dread criticism when despite all your best efforts you incur it. Instead, as I have said before, make a constant effort to always keep in your mind the image of that bright crowd of invisible spectators who witness your daily conduct; always "seek that honour which cometh from God." You cannot go forward a single step until you have become indifferent to what people will think of you. I don't need to say this over again, for I have discussed all this in an earlier chapter, that you should never try to stand out from others. Make it your goal to seek always to please God. When the world's opinion is different from God's, remember that if you follow the world, you will never be truly respectable or good or happy.

Continue to be always aware of your own desperate corruption and habitual weakness. In fact, if your eyes are really opened and your heart truly softened, if you are "hungering and thirsting after righteousness," growing deeper in your ideas of true holiness and proving the sincerity of your hope by desiring "to purify yourself even as God is pure," you will become daily more and more sensitive to your own defects and needs and weaknesses. At the same time, you will become more and more impressed with a sense of the Savior's mercy and patience. He is the one "who forgiveth all your sins, and healeth all your infirmities."

This answer seems like a strange paradox to worldly wisdom. But the reality is that your humility will grow in proportion to your growth in grace. Humility is in fact essential to Christianity; it is the quality that makes our faith live and thrive from beginning to end. When our humility grows, our faith will also flourish; but when our humility begins to fail, so will our faith. Humility will allow you to accept the gospel's offers; it will be the foundation of all your feelings and conduct, and it will be at the root of all your relationships, with God and with your fellow creatures and with yourself. And when one day you finally reach the realms of glory, your humility will be undiminished. On that day, you will "fall down; and cast your crown before the Lamb; and ascribe blessing, and honour, and glory, and power, to him that sitteth upon the throne, and to the Lamb, for ever and ever."

The practical benefits of this habitual humility are too numerous, and at the same time too obvious, for me to enumerate them all. Humility will lead you to dread anything that leads you into sin, the way you would be afraid of some infectious illness, knowing that it was a disease you were all too likely to contract. Humility prevents a thousand problems, and it answers a thousand questions about what you should do in particular circumstances in the world. You will not want to risk "grieving the Holy Spirit of God," provoking Him to withdraw His grace-giving influence.

But if you have really experienced all that I have described, I do not need to urge you to set your standards of conduct high, nor do I need to tell you to strive for complete holiness. The desire of your heart will already be to act in all things with one goal only: the favor of God. When you are controlled by this desire, the most ordinary actions of life are raised into spiritual acts of faith. This is the real golden touch that Midas should have experienced, for the touch of this transforming faith changes our entire lives to gold.

If we really want to please God, we will always seek the path that He wants for us. We will not wait lazily, satisfied that we have not refused any opportunity to do good that was forced upon us. Instead, we will pray to God for wisdom and spiritual understanding, so that we may have the insight to discern opportunities for serving Him in our world. We will be judicious in finding ways to do good, and wise as we carry out these opportunities.

Guard against the distraction of worldly cares; cultivate heavenly-mindedness and a spirit of continual prayer. Don't neglect to always watch your deceitful heart. But at the same time be active also and useful, too. Don't let your precious time be wasted by shapeless laziness. These days, even the most spiritual of us tend to have a relaxed attitude about spiritual discipline. Instead, use your time and energy wisely, as good stewards. Never be satisfied with your present achievement, but "forgetting the things which are behind," work to "press forward" with undiminished energy, running the race that is set before you without ever flagging.

176

Above all, measure your progress by how much you love God and others. "God is love"; this is the sacred essence of our faith. It warms and enlightens the heavenly world, which is the blessed seat of God's visible presence. There it shines with unclouded radiance. Here on Earth we receive some scattered beams of grace; otherwise, we would be lost in darkness and misery. An even larger portion of God's love is infused into the hearts of us who are the servants of God, who "are renewed in the divine likeness." That is why even here on Earth we demonstrate some faint traces of the image of our heavenly Father. This principle of love disposes us to yield ourselves up without reserve to the service of Him "who has bought us with the price of his own blood."

In contrast, nominal Christians' concept of spiritual practice is servile, self-centered, and mercenary. They give no more than they have to; they abstain from nothing that they can get away with. In short, they think of Christianity only as a system of restraints. They strip from it every generous and loving quality, making it almost unfit for life's ordinary social interactions. True Christians, however, don't think of themselves as satisfying some demanding creditor; instead, they see that they are discharging a debt of gratitude. That is why their obedience is not grudging and small, but measured out instead with the free and liberal hand of voluntary service.

When our motives are less generous, however, we will never act unless we are absolutely certain that we must. Gratitude, like we have already said of humility, takes away our indecision in regards to some service. We no longer wonder if we are being asked to do more than we should.

"Neither will I offer burnt-offerings unto the LORD my

God," says David, "of that which doth cost me nothing" (2 Sam. 24:24); "[The apostles] departed from the presence of the council, rejoicing that they were counted worthy to suffer shame for his name" (Acts 5:41). (See also 1 Thess. 1:6; Heb. 10:34; James 1:2; 1 Pet. 4:13–14.) These Scriptures show us what a true love for God should look like. We serve the same Lord that the apostles did, and while our love may never be put to the same severe test that theirs was, yet, if we felt the same love they did, we would surely want to act in the same spirit as they demonstrated, willing like them to deny ourselves for Christ's sake. We would not complain, as we are so apt to do, whenever we are called on to perform some act of love or to abstain from something we are inclined to do.

This principle of love regulates the true Christian's choice of companions and friends, where she is at liberty to make such a choice. It fills her with the desire to promote the physical well-being of all around her. Still more, it makes her feel compassion and an anxious concern for their spiritual welfare. If we feel indifference instead, this is one of the surest signs that our faith is weak or declining. Love brings our faith to life. In our happier times, it gives us joy and delight as we worship God; it fills us with comfort and peace, and gladness. Sometimes it even enables us "to rejoice with joy unspeakable and full of glory."

But this world is not our resting place. To the very end, we must think of ourselves as pilgrims and strangers, soldiers whose warfare ends only with death, ever struggling and combating with the powers of darkness, the temptations of the world around us, and the still more dangerous hostilities of our own internal depravity. The perpetual changes that we encounter in this world, the trials and difficulties that checker our lives, and even more, the painful and humiliating reminders of our own weaknesses, all teach us to look forward, our necks outstretched like racehorses, to that promised day when we will be completely delivered from the bondage of corruption. In that day, sorrow and sighing will flee away.

The true Christian conquers the fear of death by anticipating that blessed day. He compares this rude and troubled world, where competition and envy, anger and revenge, so vex and agitate us all, with that joyful place where love will reign undisturbed. There we will all be knit together with bonds of unbreakable friendship, and we will unite in one harmonious song of praise to the author of our shared happiness. The true Christian longs to finally see these encouraging sights; he can barely wait to enter that "blessed company."

All that I have said so far may serve to answer a common argument from nominal Christians. "You would," they say, "deny us the innocent amusements and gratifications of life. You would make our faith wear a gloomy and forbidding face, when it ought to be shining with cheerfulness and joy." This is a serious charge, so serious that although it leads me into a digression, I feel I need to answer it.

In the first place, our faith prohibits no amusement or gratification that is really innocent. The question, however, of its innocence must not be proven by the loose standards of worldly morality, but by the spirit of the Word of God. Can we pursue some enjoyment and still be conformed to the spirit of Christianity? We should have no argument concerning the true reason for recreation. Whatever form it takes, it is intended to refresh our exhausted bodies and mental powers, to restore us with renewed vigor to life's more serious occupations. That is why something that actually wears down either the body or the mind, instead of refreshing them, is not true recreation. Whatever consumes more time, money, or thought than is necessary for something that is mere amusement, that activity can hardly be approved by anyone who considers these things to be precious funds of which we are to be good stewards. Whatever directly or indirectly is likely to injure the welfare of a fellow creature can scarcely be a suitable recreation for a Christian, who is "to love his neighbour as himself." This is no diversion for anyone whose business in life is to spread happiness.

But does a Christian never relax? We shouldn't discredit God's bounty by even implying that this might be the case. He has provided us with such abundant sources of innocent enjoyment, that we should not think that we have to resort to entertainment that is unhealthy and unpleasing to Him. On the contrary, our creator is so good that He has designed the entire world to give us pleasure. Our physical and intellectual and spiritual abilities, as well as the whole creation that we see around us, are all designed each for a purpose; they are not only useful in practical ways, but they also give us joy.

> *Not content*
> *With every food of life to nourish us,*
> *You make all nature beauty to our eyes*
> *And music to our ears.*

Our maker also, in His kindness, has made us so that we can

find refreshment and pleasure even in the ordinary changes of our lives. Given that, we should be careful to wisely look for pleasure in a variety of places. If we take the recreation we need when we need it, we will be less likely to be tempted by diversions that are unhealthy to our souls.

The springs of innocent relaxation are rich and plentiful. As Christians, we relax by making moderate use of all God's gifts. Imagination and taste, the intellect and the beauties of creation, works of art and literary creations, all lie open to us. We relax with the feasts of thought, in the interactions of society, partaking of the sweets of friendship, enjoying the endearments of love, exercising with hope and trust, joy and gratitude, generosity and kindness, all the emotions that God has created for us. He designed us so that these things not only help make others happy, but they also produce our own pleasure and peace.

How little people know of true enjoyment if they can compare these delightful pleasures with the empty pleasure of dissipation or the coarse gratification of sensuality. It is no wonder, however, that the nominal Christian should reluctantly give up, one by one, the pleasures of the world; and look back upon them once he does with eyes of wistfulness and regret—because he doesn't know the true sweetness of the delights that real Christianity offers. We are more than compensated for whatever we have sacrificed in Christ's name—but the nominal Christian is unacquainted with spiritual joys.

Admittedly, when someone is first converted, she has to suffer a difficult change in her life, and it is generally a hard process for her to let go of the selfish pleasures that she has made her habit. Fear, guilt, remorse, shame, and various other feelings struggle and conflict inside her. Her desires clamor for what they are used to receiving, and habits are hard to break. She is weighed down by a load of guilt, and almost overwhelmed by the sense of her unworthiness. But these unpleasant feelings ought in fairness to be blamed on her past sins, rather than her present repentance. At any rate, this state of suffering rarely lasts very long. When the emotional gloom is the blackest, a ray of heavenly light breaks in from time to time, bringing the hope of better days. Even in this life it is usually true that "they that sow in tears shall reap in joy."

Of course, when I say that the ways of faith are ways of joy, I do not mean to deny that the Christian's internal state, through his entire life, is one of discipline and warfare. I've already pointed out several reasons, both external and internal, why this is so. But even though the Christian does have unique trials, he has even greater joys.

A little religion is, I must confess, as apt to make people gloomy as a little knowledge is to make them conceited. Perhaps this is because our faith often makes us begin to criticize our conduct, making us uneasy. It keeps us from enjoying our selfish sins the way we once did, but at the same time, if we only dabble with religion, we don't yet know the delight that true faith brings. When this happens, we are like the spies sent into Israel who brought back bad news of the land, although they had not ventured very far into it. In reality, faith will lead us to a land of promise that is full of whatever can best refresh and strengthen us on our journey through life.

Anyone who is not really a Christian will never understand all the sources of pleasure that we find in Christ. What is more, we are no longer distracted by the selfish passions and corroding cares that harass those who live in the world. Our treasure is safe from mortal accidents; we have a humble, quiet-giving hope that is based on our reconciliation with God. As we enjoy His favor, He gives us a concrete peace of mind, that the world can neither give nor take away. It is the result of our firm confidence in the infinite wisdom and goodness of God and the unceasing care and kindness of a grace-giving Savior. We have God's assurance that all things shall work together for good.

When we are flushed with youth, health, and vigor, when everything goes well and success seems to almost anticipate our wishes—then we may not feel the need for the comfort of faith. But when fortune frowns on us, or friends forsake us, when sorrow, sickness, or old age come upon us, then we can see clearly how superior faith's joys are to those selfish ones that are so apt to fly from us when we most want their help. I have never seen anything sadder than an old man who has never found out how comforting faith can be. I am moved, and at the same time disgusted, when I see him awkwardly reaching toward the pleasures of his younger years that are now beyond his reach, feebly attempting to hold on to them while they only mock his efforts and elude his grasp. To a person like this, how sad indeed is the evening of life! Everything must look sour and cheerless to him. He can neither look backward with comfort, nor forward with hope. Meanwhile, though, the Christian who has lived long years continues to rely on the promised mercy of her redeemer. She can calmly reflect that soon she will leave this world; her redemption draws near, and while her strength declines and her faculties decay, she can rest quietly on God's faithfulness. At the very entrance of the valley of the shadow of death, she can still lift up her eyes. Even though her vision may be dim and feeble, her gaze still sparkles with hope as she confidently looks forward to the moment that is coming soon when she will possess her heavenly inheritance. There at last she will grasp hold of those joys that "eye hath not seen, nor ear heard, neither have entered into the heart of man, the things which God hath prepared for them that love him" (1 Cor. 2:9).

We have never had more reason than we do today for seeking our joys in the realm where they cannot be damaged by the changes in our world. All our possessions here on Earth are fragile; they are taken from us so easily by the circumstances of life. Wealth and power and prosperity: How vulnerable they all are to life's dangers! But faith, on the other hand, hands us its best delights in the midst of our worst moments of trial: in poverty, in exile, in sickness, and in death. We may not notice how much we depend on our faith if we possess the world's riches and a position of power or influence, if we are healthy and talented and happy. But when time's rude hand sweeps all of these away, or the rough blasts of adversity blow them into destruction, then the true Christian still stands, like a tall, proud tree. Erect and vigorous, although stripped of his summer foliage, he still reveals his solid strength and durable texture.

Some Advice to Those Who Profess Their Commitment to the Gospel

In an earlier chapter we spent some time discussing the

fundamental errors of most professed Christians in our day. We pointed out that they either overlook or misunderstand the gospel's unique method for renovating our corrupted nature and for attaining every Christian grace.

But there are more mistakes everywhere you look. We all have a tendency to fly from one extreme into an opposite error. That is why I want to add another warning. I have already pointed out the worst and most common error we see in nominal Christianity today, but while I don't want us to forget to attend to this problem by prescribing heartfelt repentance and a living faith to these people as the only root and foundation for true holiness, still at the same time, we must be on guard against a mistake of another kind.

Those who have humbled themselves with penitent hearts before the cross of Christ, who accept Him as their only ground for pardon and resolve through the influences of the Holy Spirit from now on to bring forth the fruits of righteousness, these people are sometimes apt to behave as if they considered their work to be completed. They fall into the error of thinking that the initial act of repentance was all they had to do. They find, though, that they soon fall into sin again—and then they assume that another act of repentance and faith is necessary.

This is not an uncommon mistake in our day. Many Christians never get past the initial threshold of their faith. They are caught here in a constantly repeating loop of repentance. Meanwhile, they neglect the vigilant care and discipline they should be learning to exercise over their souls. They practice no self-examination, and so they never come to understand the nature, the root, and all the ramifications of their selfish sin. They have not become

185

acquainted with its secret movements, nor have they found any understanding of the things that give it strength; as a result, they have no idea what would be the most effectual methods to resist it. In a similar manner, they don't strive with persevering eagerness for grace.

And it is not unusual for the very ministers who preach the gospel's truths with faithfulness, ability, and success, to be themselves guilty of talking only about the initial steps to salvation. Over and over, their congregations hear this message, but they never learn how to discover the secret motion of inner corruption; they get no advice on the practical aspects of Christian warfare; they are not taught how to best strive against each selfish tendency of their hearts, and they receive no instruction for cultivating each grace of the Christian character.

As a result, we see far too little progress made in the lives of these Christians. We would be sorry to entertain any doubts about the sincerity of their profession, and yet we can observe no change in their temperaments, no difference in the way they use their time, and no reform in their plan for life or in their ability to resist temptation. They continue to confess that they are "miserable sinners"; this seems to be the basic tenet of their creed, and they even feel proud to avow it. They will occasionally also lament particular failings, but their confession is sometimes obviously made in order to draw forth a compliment for the very opposite virtue. Where this is not the case, we can still easily detect under their false guise of contrition a secret self-complacency. They seem to pride themselves for being so honest and candid, for showing such insight by perceiving their sins, or for being so humble as to acknowledge them.

Please don't think I am being judgmental. I speak from first-hand experience, for I have observed this same tendency in my own heart. The faults I am most apt to confess are very seldom the ones with which I should be most concerned.

When we see people caught in this trap, we must warn them that they are in danger of deceiving themselves. I want to also impress this same warning on our ministers. Let's beware lest we practice a nominal Christianity of another sort. We must remind ourselves that there is no short, easy method to achieve holiness. Instead, the business of our entire lives should be to grow in grace, continually adding one virtue to another, so that as far as we are able, we will "go on towards perfection." The Bible tells us that "he only that doeth righteousness is righteous." Unless we "bring forth the fruits of the Spirit," we have no reason to say that we have received that Spirit of Christ—and without it we are not His.

We may feel unwilling to pass an unfavorable judgment on others, and this may lead us to indulge our hope that "the root of the matter is found in them." Nevertheless, we must declare to them that they are no credit to the doctrine of Christ; instead, they disparage and discredit it. The world cannot see their secret humility, nor does it know what they do when they are alone with God, but it is acute at discerning everyday weaknesses. The world can see all too clearly that these Christians have the same eagerness in their pursuit of wealth or ambition that they ever did. What's more, they also have the same selfish taste for ostentation and display, the same ungoverned temper that we see in most human beings. So if these Christians claim to be holy and healthy and indifferent to worldly possessions, the world will only laugh at their hypocrisy. Another unfortunate result is that those in the world are apt to be hardened in their prejudices against faith; looking at these Christians' false example, the world will be less likely to accept the means God has provided for our escape from the wrath to come, and it will miss out on eternal happiness.

So if you really want to be a Christian, watch over your life and heart with unceasing care. Make an effort to learn, both from others and from books, particularly from the lives of prominent Christians, what methods have been actually found that are effective for conquering our hearts' selfish habits. Study what disciplines lead to holiness. Examine your own character and observe the private workings of your own mind. Learn about human nature. This sort of knowledge will help you to be on guard against temptations. It will also tend, above all things, to encourage the growth of humility in your heart. It will help you maintain the alert spirit and tender conscience that are so characteristic of the true Christian.

With unceasing diligence, as the apostle tells us, the servants of Christ must make their calling sure. Their work will not be thrown away; "an entrance shall" in the end "be ministered unto [them] abundantly into the everlasting kingdom of our Lord and Saviour Jesus Christ" (2 Pet. 1:11).

Some Brief Comments to Skeptics

There is another class of people, a growing class, I am afraid, in this country: that of absolute nonbelievers. I have not been addressing this book to these people, but now, since I have such sincere compassion for their sad condition, may I be permitted to ask them a few plain questions?

If you don't think that Christianity is true, don't you think it is at least worth serious consideration? Think about it. Some of our best thinkers have been convinced of its reality, men like Bacon, Milton, Locke, and Newton. These men have been admired by everyone for their deep understanding and the extent of their knowledge, for the freedom of their minds and their daring to combat existing prejudices. Can you truthfully say that you have really examined all the evidences for revelation? Have you given this subject the serious and diligent consideration it deserves?

Turning back to my original audience, I have to say that the fact is, disbelief is not generally the result of sober inquiry and deliberate preference. Instead, it is the slow result of a thoughtless life combined with prejudices and misconceptions concerning the nature of Christianity's most important doctrines and tenets.

Look at the case of young wealthy men who have been raised as nominal Christians. As children, they were carried to church, and there they became acquainted with the parts of Scripture that are contained in our public services. If their parents kept up some of the customs of better times, they were taught their catechism, and in this way they were furnished with a little more religious knowledge. After awhile, they went out from their parents' watchful eye and entered the world. There they moved forward in the path of life, whatever it might be, that had been assigned to them. They yield now to the temptations that assail them and become more or less dissipated and licentious. They never look into their Bibles; they do not enlarge their religious knowledge;

they do not even try, through reflection and study, to turn their childhood trust into an adult knowledge and rational conviction.

They travel perhaps to foreign countries, and this tends to further relax any religious habits that were bred into them as children, since they feel free to abstain from public worship when its outer forms look different from that to which they are accustomed. They return home, and usually they are either hurried around in a whirlpool of selfish pleasures, or they engage with youthful ardor in some public or professional pursuit. If they read or hear anything about Christianity, it is usually only about those tenets that are subjects of controversy. When they do attend church, what reaches their ears may sometimes impress them with an idea of Christianity's purity, but heard out of context, it confuses and offends them, suggesting various doubts and objections that further acquaintance with the Scripture would remove. More and more, their only knowledge of Christianity is of the difficulties it contains.

As a result, sometimes they may be tempted by an ambition to show that they are superior to what they think is ignorant prejudice. Always, they are prompted by the natural pride of the human heart to free themselves from any subjection to the dogmas imposed on them by Christianity. They may be disgusted by the immoral lives of some professed Christians or by the weakness and absurdity of others. Many doubts and suspicions like these spring up within them.

These doubts enter into their minds at first almost imperceptibly; they exist only as vague and indistinct assumptions that lack any precise shape or the substance of a well-formed opinion. At first, probably, they are even offended and startled by the intrusion of these thoughts. By degrees, however, they get used to thinking this way; the mind grows more familiar with these doubts. They have a confused sense that they would like to see their doubts proved. As a result, the mental impression dug by these questions becomes deeper—not because they have been reinforced by fresh arguments, but merely because they have occupied the mind for a longer time. As they increase in force, they creep out and extend themselves. In the end, they diffuse themselves over the whole concept of faith, and their possession of the entire mind is undisturbed.

I don't mean to say that this process is always the same for everyone. But speaking generally, this might be realistically termed the natural history of skepticism. You know the truth of what I'm saying if you've watched the growth of disbelief in the people around you. What is more, it is confirmed by the written lives of some of the most prominent nonbelievers. Their own accounts of themselves support what I have observed. We find that these authors once gave a sort of implicit hereditary assent to the truth of Christianity—and then, using a dangerous perversion of language, they "awakened from the sleep of ignorance." At what moment did the "light of truth" beam in on them and dissipate the darkness? The period during which they lost their faith is never marked by any such definite boundary. Reason, thought, and inquiry had little or nothing to do with it. Having for many years lived careless lives, associating with companions equally careless, they at last reached maturity in their lack of faith. But it did not come to them through study and reflection, but rather through the lapse of time. Let me point out, however, that when the process is

191

reversed and they are converted back to faith, it is almost always a much more rational process. Something awakens them intellectually so that they are open to new concepts. They examine, they consider, they reflect, and at length they acknowledge Christianity, based on what they deem to be sufficient grounds.

From what I have said, a lack of faith appears plainly to be the offspring of prejudice. Its continued success can be mainly ascribed to the depravity of the moral character. This fact is confirmed by the undeniable truth that a lack of faith in society is not the natural fruit of studious discussions, but of a selfish and destructive age. It spreads itself through our thoughts as general morals decline, and it is embraced with less apprehension when people see so many around them practicing the same lack of faith.

This alone may be a good argument for the reality of revelation. Christianity's critics often claim that we are the victims of ignorance and irrationality. However, as we have seen, the opposite is often the case.

In our own day, our lack of faith is not built on the philosophy and writings of the ancient pagan writers. We can claim no such intellectual source for our disbelief. Instead, the progress of luxury and the decay of morals are at the root of our problems. If we can trace our problems at all to the works of skeptical writers, it is not through intellectual argument and discussion that they have had any effect, but through the sarcasm and witticisms that have worked on weak minds or on nominal Christians, bringing gradually into contempt opinions that in their case only rested on blind respect and the prejudices of education. I think I can therefore safely say that a lack of faith is in general a disease of the heart more than of the mind.

If revelation was attacked only by reason and argument, it would have little to fear. The literary enemies of Christianity have been seldom read. They made some stir in their day; during their brief span of existence they were noisy and obnoxious; but like the locusts of the east, which for awhile obscure the sky and destroy everything that is green, they were soon swept away and forgotten. Their very names can scarcely be found in our libraries.

What I have said about the lack of faith in general can most likely be extended to accurately apply as well to those who deny the fundamental doctrines of the gospel.

In the path that we just traced from nominal orthodoxy to an absolute lack of faith, Unitarianism may be called a sort of halfway house, a stage on the journey. Some people may sometimes remain at this stage, but often they only pause for awhile and then continue on their way.

I am aware that I may be criticized for using this controversial term. Many orthodox Christians also believe in the unity of the divine nature, and they may refer to themselves as being Unitarian in their belief. I don't want to be guilty of labeling others unjustly. However, I am referring to the term "Unitarianism" as it has been popularly used, and I want to refute the arguments commonly used by the people who themselves claim this title.

The Unitarian teachers by no means claim to absolve their followers from the unbending strictness of Christian morality. They prescribe a love for God that dominates all life and a habitual spirit of devotion. However, people who seek refuge in this form of faith seem to go there because they want a watered-down sort of faith; they want the joys of

Christianity without the difficult doctrines. In particular, most of them seem to want to escape the Bible's command to be separate from the world, a unique and special people. They prefer to remain at one with the world's philosophies.

When Unitarianism comes out of the intellect rather than the heart, it seems to often be produced by a confused idea of the difficulties—or, as they call them, the impossibilities—that orthodox Christianity is supposed to contain. I don't want to enter this controversy, but I do want to point out that both the Deists and the Unitarians have the advantage of being on the offensive when they attack orthodox Christianity. They refer to their arguments against the truth of Christianity's fundamental doctrines as powerful ones, and then call upon people to abandon these "unsupportable" positions. But if you feel disposed to yield to this assault, call to mind that God has been pleased to create the world in such a way that we can argue against almost anything. We can even argue that there is no God at all if we so choose.

Because of this, it makes no sense to throw away a proposition simply because arguments exist against it. What we should do instead is compare the arguments in favor of faith with the arguments against it. Which hold the most weight? What are we left with if we abandon faith? Do we find ourselves left with even more difficulties than we had before when it comes to explaining the realities of our world? In short, consider carefully all the arguments before you make any decisions.

Christianity has not gone to the same efforts to promote its arguments that the Unitarians have. If they were attacked as they have attacked orthodoxy, and asked to defend their tenets, I doubt they would be able to keep their ground so well. In short, we can find no watered-down alternative to Christianity that can be rationally supported. If we have abandoned Christianity, then we must logically abandon all its forms. We must abandon any hope we have of finding the comfort of faith without its demands.

Besides the Unitarians who profess to reject the Bible as divine revelation, there is another class of people, a growing one, that we might call half-nonbelievers. These can be found in various degrees as they approach a total lack of faith. Their thinking, however, is clearly irrational. They hear many people assert the truth of Christianity, and they hear many others deny it; as a result, they take for themselves a strange sort of middle ground, never bothering to reflect seriously enough to realize that this is something that must be either true or false. Instead, they tell themselves that there must be something to it, while at the same time they consider that it cannot be as true as orthodox Christians insist. They don't accept any of the Bible's actual doctrines, and yet they assume that they believe enough to get by, that their minimal faith will allow them to squeak into heaven should Christianity turn out to be true.

Again, let me remind you that there is no middle road. If you look into your Bible, and you do not make up your mind to absolutely reject its authority, then you must admit that you have no grounds for hoping to escape the punishment that the Bible predicts. Don't think that your guilt is so little that God will not bother with it. It is ludicrous to think you can trifle with God's patience, ignoring both His invitations and His threats, refusing the offer of His Spirit of grace and the precious blood of the redeemer. Scripture warns, "How shall we escape if we neglect so great salvation?" "It shall be more tolerable for the land of Sodom and Gomorrha in the day of judgment" (Matt. 10:15) than for those who voluntarily shut their eyes against the full light that heaven's bounty has poured down on them.

These half-nonbelievers are even worse than downright skeptics, for they remain in a state of careless uncertainty, without even trying to discover the truth or falsehood of revelation. If they admit that there is even a chance that the Bible is true, then they are obligated to study this possibility more closely. But for both them and for skeptics alike, so many proofs for Christianity are available that it is inexcusable in our day to reject Christ. God's bounty has seen to it that the more a lack of faith poisons our society, the more He spreads His powerful antidotes throughout our world.

These nonbelievers are infatuated with blind trust. They will not give up Christianity's rewards, and yet they think that they will be exempt from its punishments. But that is not the case; they must stand the risk of their inevitable encounter with God; their eternal happiness or misery is suspended on the outcome of that meeting. (For more on this line of thinking, let me recommend to you Pascal's *Thoughts on Religion*. While I do not agree with every part of this book, I find it to be a deep and highly valuable work.)

Can you imagine how it must feel to open your eyes in the world to come and be convinced too late of the awful reality of our impending ruin? May the mercy and the power of God awaken us from our dangerous slumber, while we still have life! There is still time for repentance.

Some Advice to True Christians

In the course of this work I have said much in passing to those of you who really deserve the name of true Christians. You are the most important members of our community (and I doubt this claim would be disputed by any experienced politician). Today, as faith falls out of fashion, this is more true than ever before, both in our own nation and in all of Europe. So I ask you now to seriously weigh the important role that you have; consider all the various responsibilities that enforce this role.

If we read the most intelligent accounts of foreign countries, we are convinced that faith and the standard of morals are declining everywhere, abroad even more rapidly than in our own country. But the fact that conditions may be worse in other countries is no reason for us to be complacent here in our own nation. The progress of nonbelief and the decay of morals at home are serious enough to alarm us all. They forebode the worst consequences, unless we find some remedy to the growing evil.

We can depend only on you who are true Christians to perform this important service. Faith's cause requires zeal, and only you can feel it. The people who try to work change in our country will be accused of being strange and inappropriate; only you will dare to encounter this criticism. The effort will require unity and perseverance; we can hope to find those qualities only in you who have true faith in Christ.

I call on all of you who are true Christians, then, to work together earnestly to prove the worth of your profession, putting to silence the empty ridicule of ignorant objectors. Boldly stand up for the cause of Christ in an age when so many who bear the name of Christ are ashamed of Him. On your shoulders rests your country's fate; it is up to you to suspend its fall. In the end, however, we can never be certain of the political outcome of our actions—but nevertheless, without a doubt, restoring the influence of faith and raising the moral standard will have sure and radical benefits for us all.

Be active, useful, generous toward others; show yourselves to be moderate and self-denying in all things. Never be lazy; avoid this sin as much as you would any more obvious one. When God blesses you with affluence, withdraw yourselves from all empty competitions. Show yourselves to be modest in your demeanor, and never put on any affectation that would make you stand out in some way from others. At the same time, don't be a slave to fashion; instead, set an example for others by using your money for less selfish, more noble purposes than mere show. In other words, don't waste your money on impressing people with your clothes or your vehicles or any other ostentatious sign of wealth. Be moderate in everything. Set your hearts on higher goals than anything that this world has to offer. You will find that you possess within you all that you need for satisfaction and comfort. Meanwhile, the world seeks for this contentment in all the empty, selfish pleasures, and yet it never finds it.

Cultivate a spirit of goodwill for everyone. Join in friendly fellowship with all people of faith, whatever their sect or denomination. If you find you differ from them in some areas, remember that so long as you agree on faith's central doctrine, the rest is nonessential. Respect people of real spirituality wherever they are found, and encourage others to grow in their faith. Do all you can to help revive and spread the influence of faith and virtue. Pray earnestly and constantly that your efforts will be successful. Ask God to be patient with us, allowing us to continue the priceless privilege of Christianity's vital practice.

Pray continually for your country. The governor of the universe, who has told us He is a God who hears the prayers of His servants, may answer our intercessions and avert for awhile our ruin. He may even continue to grant us those earthly blessings that we have always enjoyed so abundantly. The world may only acknowledge the natural operation of natural causes; they may not admit that faith and morality promote the well-being of the community. When they read of Christians' service to their nation, they may respond with either a smile of complacent pity or a sneer of supercilious contempt—and yet in the end, your prayers may bring real change to our country. Nonbelievers will think you are no different than the terrified inhabitants of Sicily who brought out the image of their favorite saint to protect them from the destructive ravages of Etna—but you will know better. Scripture tells us that God favors the nations to which His servants belong; according to the Bible, God's people have often been the unknown and unhonored instruments that drew down on their country the blessings of safety and prosperity.

I don't want to be an example of that same reluctance to acknowledge my faith that I have criticized in others—so let me boldly say that I firmly believe our country's problems are all caused, either directly or indirectly, by the decline of faith and morality in our nation. The only solid hope for our country's well-being does not depend as much on our fleets and armies, nor on the wisdom of our rulers, nor the spirit of our people, as it does on faith and love for the gospel of Christ. I humbly trust that the intercession of real Christians is still so great that God may look upon us with favor for their sake.

I also want to ask all of you who are real Christians to pray that God will use this book to further the cause of true faith. God can make use of even the weakest effort—and I will be honored if even one person should be awakened from his false security by reading this book. Or if even a single true Christian is encouraged to live a life of greater usefulness, then I will consider my effort to be worthwhile.

I hope no one will assume that I have no knowledge on which to base my assumptions. I know what I am talking about. My responsibilities in life lead me into direct contact with the policies of our nation. As a result, I feel I have a serious obligation to my acquaintances and friends. I am truly concerned for the welfare of my fellow creatures.

Europe today is full of a false philosophy that is pre- ferred to the light of revelation. A lack of faith is every- where, lifting its head without any shame as it enters in broad daylight every human activity. The practical conse- quences are just what we might expect: Selfishness and sin prevail without restraint. But here in our own country, let us make a sanctuary, a land of faith and spirituality where the blessings of Christianity may still be enjoyed; where the name of the redeemer will still be honored; where human- ity can see what faith in Jesus really means and what are its blessed effects; and where, if the mercy of God allows it, faith and comfort can spread out of our boundaries, into the surrounding countries, and finally to the world at large.

NOTES

Chapter Two
1. Robin Furneaux, *William Wilberforce* (London: Hamish Hamilton, 1974), 8.
2. John Pollock, *Wilberforce* (New York: St. Martin's Press, 1977), 6.
3. Garth Lean, *God's Politician: William Wilberforce's Struggle* (Colorado Springs, Colo.: Helmers and Howard, [March 1989]), 12.
   Furneaux, 11.

Chapter Four
1. Pollock, 27.
2. Furneaux, 30.

Chapter Five
1. Ibid., 36.

Chapter Six
1. Ibid., 37–38.
2. Lean, 37.

Chapter Seven
1. Pollock, 41.
2. Ibid.
3. Lean, 42.
4. Ibid., 44.
5. Pollock, 50.
6. Ibid., 51.
7. Furneaux, 70.

8. Ibid., 70.
9. Pollock, 53.
10. Ibid.

Chapter Eight
1. Furneaux, 73–75.
2. Lean, 51.

Chapter Nine
1. Pollock, 47.
2. Lean, 73–77.
3. Pollock, 61.
4. Lean, 88–91.

Chapter Ten
1. Furneaux, 99.
2. Pollock, 119–120.
3. Ibid., 118.
4. Lean, 106.

Chapter Eleven
1. Mark O. Hatfield, in William Wilberforce, *Real Christianity: Contrasted with the Prevailing Religious System* (Portland, Ore.: Multnomah Press, 1982), xvi.
2. Pollock, 122.
3. Ibid., 130–131.
4. Furneaux, 184.

Chapter Twelve
1. Pollock, 47.
2. Ibid., 82.

Chapter Thirteen
1. Furneaux, 95.
2. Ibid., 109.
3. Ibid., 111.

Chapter Fourteen
1. Wilberforce, 1.
2. Ibid., 30.
3. Ibid., 41.
4. Ibid., 130–131.
5. Furneaux, 151–152.
6. Pollock, 149.
7. Lean, 134.

Chapter Fifteen
1. Furneaux, 162.

Chapter Sixteen
1. Ibid., 250.
2. Ibid., 253.

Chapter Seventeen
1. Ibid., 314.
2. Ibid., 315.
3. Pollock, 267.
4. Ibid., 290.

Chapter Eighteen
1. Furneaux, 455.
2. Ibid., 456.